The Printer's Trial

The Printer's Trial

The Case of John Peter Zenger and the Fight for a Free Press

Gail Jarrow

CALKINS CREEK BOOKS

Honesdale, Pennsylvania

LIBRARY OF CONGRESS CATALOGING-IN-PUBLICATION DATA
Jarrow, Gail.
The printer's trial : the case of John Peter Zenger
and the fight for a free press / by Gail Jarrow.—1st ed.
p. cm.
Includes bibliographical references.
ISBN-13: 978-1-59078-432-7 (hardcover : alk. paper)
1. Zenger, John Peter, 1697–1746—Trials, litigation, etc. 2. Trials
(Seditious libel)—New York (State)—New York.
3. Freedom of the press—United States—History—Sources. I. Title.
KF223.Z4J37 2006
345.73'0231—dc22
2006000772

CALKINS CREEK BOOKS
An Imprint of Boyds Mills Press, Inc.
A Highlights Company

815 Church Street
Honesdale, Pennsylvania 18431

For Robert, who took me along to Peter Zenger's
old neighborhood one April day

And for my mother, who took me to historical sites during
my childhood and nurtured the curiosity that
—on the same April day—
led me up the steps of Federal Hall

Numb. II.

THE
New-York Weekly JOURNAL

Containing the freſheſt Advices, Foreign, and Domeſtick.

MUNDAY November 12, 1733.

Mr. Zenger.

INcert the following in your next, and you'll oblige your Friend,

CATO.

Mira temporum felicitas ubi ſentiri qiiæ velis, & quæ ſentias dicere licit.

Tacit.

THE Liberty of the Preſs is a Subject of the greateſt Importance, and in which every Individual is as much concern'd as he is in any other Part of Liberty: Therefore it will not be improper to communicate to the Publick the Sentiments of a late excellent Writer upon this Point. ſuch is the Elegance and Perſpicuity of his Writings, ſuch the inimitable Force of his Reaſoning, that it will be difficult to ſay any Thing new that he has not ſaid, or not to ſay that much worſe which he has ſaid.

There are two Sorts of Monarchies, an abſolute and a limited one. In the firſt, the Liberty of the Preſs can never be maintained, it is inconſiſtent with it; for what abſolute Monarch would ſuffer any Subject to animadvert on his Actions, when it is in his Power to declare the Crime, and to nominate the Puniſhment? This would make it very dangerous to exerciſe ſuch a Liberty. Beſides the Object againſt which thoſe Pens muſt be directed, is

their Sovereign, the ſole ſupream Magiſtrate; for there being no Law in thoſe Monarchies, but the Will of the Prince, it makes it neceſſary for his Miniſters to conſult his Pleaſure, before any Thing can be undertaken: He is therefore properly chargeable with the Grievances of his Subjects, and what the Miniſter there acts being in Obedience to the Prince, he ought not to incur the Hatred of the People; for it would be hard to impute that to him for a Crime, which is the Fruit of his Allegiance, 'and for refuſing which he might incur the Penalties of Treaſon. Beſides, in an abſolute Monarchy, the Will of the Prince being the Law, a Liberty of the Preſs to complain of Grievances would be complaining againſt the Law, and the Conſtitution, to which they have ſubmitted, or have been obliged to ſubmit; and therefore, in one Senſe, may be ſaid to deſerye Puniſhment, So that under an abſolute Monarchy, I ſay, ſuch a Liberty is inconſiſtent with the Conſtitution, having no proper Subject in Politics, on which it might be exercis'd, and if exercis'd would incur a certain Penalty.

But in a limited Monarchy, as *England* is, our Laws are known, fixed, and eſtabliſhed. They are the ſtreight Rule and ſure Guide to direct the King, the Miniſters, and other his Subjects: And therefore an Offence againſt the Laws is ſuch an Offence againſt the Conſtitution as ought to receive a proper adequate Puniſhment; the ſeveral Conſti.

The New-York Weekly Journal *The front page of the newspaper's second issue, published November 12, 1733.*

Contents

The true Sons of Liberty

And Supporters of the Non-Importation Agreement,

ARE determined to refent any the leaft Infult or Menace offer'd to any one or more of the feveral Committees appointed by the Body at Faneuil-Hall, and chaftife any one or more of them as they deferve; and will alfo fupport the Printers in any Thing the Committees fhall defire them to print.

☞ AS a Warning to any one that fhall affront as aforefaid, upon fure Information given, one of thefe Advertifements will be pofted up at the Door or Dwelling-Houfe of the Offender.

Down with the British! *After the 1735 Zenger trial, colonial printers enjoyed the freedom to print broadsides, pamphlets, and newspapers that criticized the British government. This one-page broadside was published in Boston in 1768 by the Sons of Liberty, a secretive group of workers and tradesmen, including many printers. In the years leading up to the American Revolution, Sons of Liberty groups from all thirteen colonies worked together to resist British control. The Non-Importation Agreement mentioned in this broadside is an example of this resistance. The Agreement, supported by the Sons, banned the sale of British goods in Boston.*

Introduction

John Peter Zenger was an unlikely hero. He had come to the American colonies as a young German immigrant with little education. He trained to be a printer, but he was not an especially skillful one. Yet the events of 1732–35 pushed Zenger into history.

A new British governor arrived in New York in 1732 to rule the province. He was unpopular with the colonists, and a group of New Yorkers decided to oppose him. The next year, they asked Peter Zenger to print their criticisms of the governor in a weekly newspaper.

Zenger had struggled for seven years to build his printing business in New York City. This was a good opportunity for him. But when he agreed to print the four-page *New-York Weekly Journal,* he thrust himself into a political storm. The governor was outraged by what he read in the newspaper. Soon Zenger found himself locked in a drafty jail cell, accused of printing material that threatened the government.

The printer's legal battle and trial became famous. The outcome cracked open the door for a free press in the American colonies. It helped make possible the printing of pamphlets and newspapers that later rallied colonists toward revolution and freedom from British rule.

The Zenger case has affected the attitudes of generations of Americans, including Thomas Jefferson, who drafted the Declaration of Independence and served as the third president of the United States. Jefferson wrote to a friend in 1787:

"The basis of our governments being the opinion of the people, the very first object should be to keep that right; and were it left to me to decide whether we should have a government without newspapers, or newspapers without a government, I should not hesitate a moment to prefer the latter."

More than fifty years after Peter Zenger's arrest, the Bill of Rights guaranteed citizens the freedom to criticize their government in the press. Today a free press continues to be an important part of American democracy.

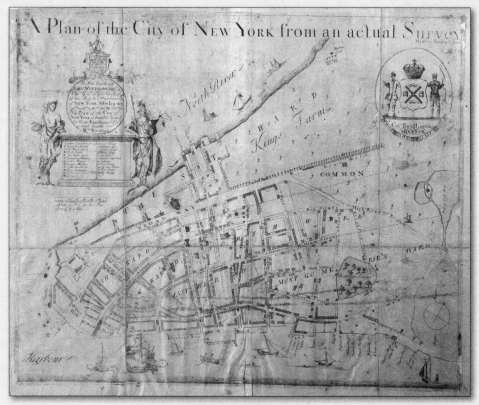

Where It All Happened—New York in the 1730s This map of the City of New York, published in 1731, was based on a survey by James Lyne and printed by William Bradford. Only three original copies of the map are known to exist, including this one from the New York Public Library's collection. It shows street names and major landmarks, such as City Hall and Fort George. The area, at the lower end of Manhattan, is only part of today's New York City.

The Characters in the Case

James Alexander—Political opponent of Governor Cosby; editor of the *New-York Weekly Journal*; lawyer for John Peter Zenger.

William Bradford—New York printer who taught Zenger the printing trade; official government printer and publisher of the *New-York Gazette*.

John Chambers—Court-appointed lawyer who took over Zenger's case after his original attorneys were disbarred.

Cadwallader Colden—Member of the Provincial Council and supporter of the Morrisites.

Governor William Cosby—British governor of the provinces of New York and New Jersey.

James De Lancey—Chief justice of the New York Supreme Court; one of two judges to preside over the Zenger trial.

Andrew Hamilton—Philadelphia lawyer who represented Zenger in court on the day of the famous trial.

Francis Harison—Member of the Provincial Council; wrote articles for the *Gazette* praising Cosby and attacking the *New-York Weekly Journal*.

Lewis Morris—New York politician who headed the Morrisite Party opposing Governor Cosby; chief justice of New York Supreme Court until dismissed by Governor Cosby; helped start the *New-York Weekly Journal*.

Lewis Morris, Jr.—Son of Lewis Morris; a politician and member of the Morrisite Party.

William Smith—One of Zenger's lawyers; part of the group that founded and wrote for the *New-York Weekly Journal*.

Rip Van Dam—Longtime member of the Provincial Council; acting governor for one year until Governor Cosby arrived in New York; his lawsuit with Cosby ignited a political struggle between the Morrisites and Cosby.

John Peter Zenger—New York printer who published and printed the *New-York Weekly Journal*; arrested and imprisoned for the crime of seditious libel.

1738 Pamphlet About Zenger's Trial *The first page from the account of Zenger's trial, written by James Alexander. This edition of* A Brief Narrative *was published in 1738 by Boston printer Thomas Fleet (1685–1758). Fleet also published the first American book of nursery rhymes in 1719, called* Songs for the Nursery, or Mother Goose's Melodies for Children.

A CHANGE IN THE CALENDAR

In the early eighteenth century, Great Britain and its colonies followed a calendar that differs from the one used today. The calendar year began in the American colonies on March 25. In 1752, this calendar was changed so that January 1 became the first day of the year. Whenever January, February, or March dates appear in this book, the modern date is indicated behind the one used at the time of the Zenger case.

To the Reader

This is the story about events that occurred nearly three hundred years ago. In the 1700s, there were no cameras or voice recorders to document important moments. How do we know what people during that time thought, said, and did?

To uncover the truth about the past, historians rely on evidence that has survived, such as the written word. Sometimes no evidence exists, and historians have to make guesses about what happened. They are careful about doing this because it is easy to guess wrong. The best historians prefer to stick with what they know.

What they know about the John Peter Zenger case comes from several sources. These include court documents, government papers, and newspapers from the 1700s. An account of Zenger's trial by one of his lawyers, James Alexander, sheds more light on the case. Letters written by major characters reveal some of their thoughts and actions.

This information provides an incomplete picture, however. Letters and documents may reflect a one-sided view of events. Some papers have surely been lost or destroyed over the centuries. Since political plans and business deals were often made face-to-face, there is no record of them.

Still, the existing evidence puts to rest several myths. For example, some people have claimed that John Peter Zenger single-handedly started and wrote the *New-York Weekly Journal*. It is true that a few colonial printers such as Benjamin Franklin are known to have authored the material in their newspapers. But historians have found no evidence that Zenger wrote the essays or articles in the *Journal*. He probably lacked the education and knowledge to have written the intellectual essays. In addition, his English skills were likely not strong since he was a German immigrant.

Many of the *Journal*'s essays have been found among James Alexander's handwritten personal papers. This proves that he was their author. Letters and other papers strongly hint at the identities of additional authors, including William Smith and Lewis Morris.

Another myth is that John Peter Zenger led the battle against the corrupt governor, William Cosby. Colonial records rarely mention Zenger's name. This indicates that he was not an influential leader of the time. On the other hand, many documents show that Alexander, Smith, and Morris were behind the political fight with Cosby.

What you read here is based on the evidence known today. Someday a lost letter or hidden document may be found that changes that view. Until new facts surface, this is what historians believe happened.

A View of FORT GEORGE with the CITY of NEW YORK from the SW.

Fort George A View of Fort George with the City of New York from the SW [Southwest], *as it looked in 1736. Engraved by Carwitham. Built by the Dutch, the fort at New York City's southern end protected it from attack by sea. The British took over the fort when they gained control of New York in 1664. In 1732, it bore the name of Great Britain's King George II. Besides housing soldiers, Fort George was the home of the British governor and the site of official events and Provincial Council meetings.*

ONE

Sparks Fly

"I had more trouble . . . then I could have imagined"

AUGUST 1732: THE GOVERNOR ARRIVES

As the well-dressed, middle-aged man stepped ashore, most of New York City's fifteen hundred houses were dark. Although it was ten o'clock at night, a welcoming committee greeted the man at the dock. After all, he was the most powerful person in the province—the new British governor, William Cosby.

Governor Cosby was weary after a nearly two-month-long voyage across the Atlantic Ocean from England. So the gentlemen of the welcoming committee led him to the nearby governor's house inside Fort George.

Late the next morning, August 2, 1732, the new governor walked several blocks along the cobblestone streets from the fort to City Hall. Parading with him past brick houses and businesses were soldiers, politicians, and merchants. It was Governor Cosby's official introduction to the city and province of New York.

The New York colonists had gotten along well with recent governors. They hoped that Governor Cosby would be fair and reasonable. But within days, there were hints that trouble loomed. Rumors about Cosby's greed and dishonesty in his previous position had earlier reached New York from England. The colonists soon would see for themselves that the rumors were true.

One of Governor Cosby's first duties was to meet with the twenty-six members of the New York Assembly. The Assembly voted to pay the governor's salary for a five-year period, which it had done for previous governors.

Not good enough, said Cosby. He wanted extra payment for his efforts while he waited in England to receive his official instructions from the Board of Trade. During those months before he sailed for America, Cosby claimed that he worked to

GOVERNOR WILLIAM COSBY (1690–1735/36)

Born in Ireland, William Cosby had been a colonel in the Royal Irish Regiment. He was not well educated or intelligent, but he married into a powerful British family. His wife's brother was the Earl of Halifax, a member of the King's Privy Council. Her cousin was the Duke of Newcastle, who was the influential secretary of state in charge of the colonies. The duke was responsible for assigning colonial positions, such as governorships. Through these family connections, Cosby was awarded the governorship of New York and New Jersey.

Cosby saw his new position in the American colonies as a way to get rich. He had already shown his greed as governor of Minorca, an island off the coast of Spain. While there, he had illegally seized the property of a merchant. Later, Cosby was forced to pay the damages, which put him in debt. He hoped to replenish his fortunes as a governor in the American colonies. Once he arrived in New York, his greed, quick temper, and arrogance made him an unpopular governor.

COLONIAL MONEY

In 1732, the American colonies used the British system of money. A pound (abbreviated with the symbol £) was the basic unit. Twenty shillings made a pound, and twelve pence made a shilling. One pound in New York colonial money in 1732 would be worth about $85 today.

prevent passage of the Molasses Act, a law being considered in the British Parliament. This law would hurt New York and the rest of the colonies by adding a high tax to molasses and sugar coming from the West Indies.

But many of the assemblymen weren't impressed by Cosby's claim to have worked against the Act. They doubted that he had the power to influence Parliament. So at first, the Assembly agreed to pay Cosby a bonus of only £750 (750 pounds).

Cosby was insulted by the amount, which he considered too little. He invited to dinner some of the assemblymen who had voted against giving him more money. After dinner, he reportedly damned them and asked them "why they did not make their Present in pounds shillings & Pennies . . . "

The governor demanded still more, despite the fact that the king's orders made it illegal for him to take a gift from the Assembly. In the end, the Assembly gave in and voted to add another £250 to the governor's bonus, for a total of £1000.

As time went on, Cosby's actions convinced many New Yorkers that the governor was more interested in making money for himself than in helping them. As governor, he had the power to give land to settlers. Cosby demanded one-third share of each land grant he made. Some colonists felt that he also abused his power by increasing fees on land titles and pocketing the money himself.

New York was small enough that reports of Cosby's behavior spread among its citizens. Many began to lose respect for him. Yet the new governor didn't seem to care what the colonists thought. The people annoyed him, and he didn't try to hide his feelings.

In October, Cosby wrote to the Duke of Newcastle in London, who was in charge of the American colonies: "I had more trouble to manige these people then I could have imagined, however for this time I have done pritty well with them."

NOVEMBER 1732: A FIGHT OVER MONEY

Governor Cosby wasn't as adept in dealing with New Yorkers as he thought. He soon offended them again.

It started over money. During the thirteen months before Cosby arrived in New York, a temporary governor had run the province. He was Rip Van Dam, the

George II (1683–1760), king of Great Britain from 1727 to 1760.

Rip Van Dam (1660–1749) was born to a Dutch family in Albany, New York. After moving to New York City as a young man, he became a successful merchant involved in the West Indies trade. Van Dam was a member of the New York Provincial Council for thirty-three years.

WHO RAN THE COLONY OF NEW YORK?

In 1732, the American colonies were under the rule of Great Britain and its **king**, George II. The king's advisors were called the **Privy Council**. The advisor responsible for running the American colonies was the **secretary of state** for the Southern Department. At that time, the Duke of Newcastle held this position.

Working with the secretary of state was the **Board of Trade**. It reported on problems and disputes in the colonies and regulated their trade. Based on recommendations from the secretary and Board of Trade, the king appointed a **governor** to enforce English law in each colony. Until 1738, the colonies of New York and New Jersey shared a governor.

New York's governor received his instructions from the Board of Trade. With the Board's approval, the governor appointed colonial officials, including supreme court judges and the members of the **Provincial Council**. The governor also chose county and city judges and sheriffs.

The Provincial Council, which had twelve members, acted as the upper house of the colonial legislature. It advised the governor and gave its consent to the governor's appointments. Council members often remained in their posts through the terms of several governors. A governor could not remove a council member without approval from the British government in London.

New York voters were allowed to elect members to the **Assembly**, the lower house of the legislature. The Assembly decided how colonial taxes would be spent, such as how much the governor was paid. Laws passed by the Assembly had to be approved by the governor and the British government. In addition, the governor had the power to prevent the Assembly from meeting.

Voters elected leaders, such as the men on New York City's **Common Council**, to run their towns and cities. Only white male property holders could vote or serve on a jury.

president of the Provincial Council. Van Dam had taken over the duties after the previous governor died in office. The Council had voted to pay Van Dam the salary that Cosby would have earned had he been there to do the job.

In November, Cosby announced that he should be paid from the time of the previous governor's death. He wanted half of what Van Dam had earned as acting governor. Van Dam agreed to split his "acting" governor's salary, but only under one condition: Cosby had to share *his* income as "appointed" governor in England during the previous year.

Van Dam said that he had earned no more than about £2000 as acting governor. He calculated that Cosby had earned £6400 during the same period. Therefore, argued the crafty Van Dam, Governor Cosby owed him money.

Cosby lost his temper—something the governor did often. Rip Van Dam refused to give in. Van Dam was a wealthy man and probably didn't need the money Cosby had demanded. But he resented the way in which Governor Cosby kept forcing New Yorkers to pay him more. If the new governor wanted to pick a fight, Van Dam was ready for battle.

The governor decided to sue Van Dam for the money. This created a problem for Cosby, however. Under English law, a jury of colonists would decide the court case. Seventy-two-year-old Rip Van Dam was a popular and well-known colonial leader. Cosby realized that a jury of New Yorkers would never force Van Dam to pay back a British governor.

What Cosby did next unleashed more public resentment against him. Using his power as governor, he set up a special court in which three supreme court judges would decide his case without a jury. Since two of the judges were Cosby's allies, the governor expected to win his lawsuit.

March–August 1733: The Fire Is Ignited

Cosby hadn't counted on the chief justice of the Supreme Court, sixty-one-year-old Lewis Morris. Morris believed that Englishmen everywhere had a right to a jury trial. He did not think a colonial supreme court should be used as a special court without a jury.

JUDGE JAMES DE LANCEY (1703–1760)
JUDGE FREDERICK PHILIPSE (1695–1751)

When Governor Cosby arrived in New York, the Supreme Court had three judges—Chief Justice Lewis Morris, James De Lancey, and Frederick Philipse. Morris's harsh words toward his two colleagues during the Van Dam case had just as much to do with politics as it did with legal opinion. The De Lancey and Philipse families were longtime political opponents of Lewis Morris. James De Lancey's father and Frederick Philipse's uncle were leaders in the Assembly who often disagreed with Morris.

James De Lancey became one of the most powerful officeholders in the New York colony. In 1729, he joined the Provincial Council, a position he held for twenty-four years. At age twenty-eight De Lancey joined the Supreme Court. Two years later Governor Cosby appointed him as chief justice, a post he held until his death.

Frederick Philipse was educated in England before returning to the colonies as a young man. He inherited a huge New York estate from his grandfather, making him a wealthy man. Philipse joined the Assembly in 1726 and the Supreme Court in 1731. He served on both until his death.

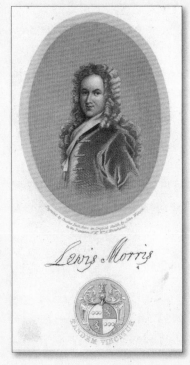

LEWIS MORRIS (1671–1746)

Lewis Morris was born in New York City. His family owned large parcels of land in New York and New Jersey, making him one of the wealthiest men in the two provinces. He owned dozens of slaves, who worked his estates and his iron mines.

A tall man with a stern manner, Morris commanded respect. But as one of his allies, Cadwallader Colden, later wrote: "He was far from being a popular man. Nor was his Temper fitted to gain popularity."

Morris had a thirst for knowledge. His library had nearly as many books as Harvard College. He studied literature, languages, law, politics, history, science, and philosophy. Ambitious and political, Morris had been active in governments of both New York and New Jersey for many years before Governor Cosby arrived. His son, Lewis Morris, Jr. (1698–1762), also held political office.

Morris had a personal stake in the argument, too. New York shared its British governor with New Jersey. As president of the New Jersey Provincial Council, Lewis Morris had acted as New Jersey governor during the year before Cosby arrived, just as Rip Van Dam had in New York. Morris expected Cosby eventually to demand half of *his* salary, too, though it was much less than Van Dam's.

When Morris announced that the Supreme Court should not be used as a special court in the Van Dam case, the other two judges—James De Lancey and Frederick Philipse—disagreed. In court, Morris called their opinions "mean, weak and futile." He said that they were siding with Cosby instead of following the law. Judge Morris stormed from the courtroom, refusing to let Cosby's lawsuit against Van Dam be heard.

A furious Cosby responded by attacking Morris's honesty. He sent Morris a message, saying that he "depended neither upon his [Morris's] Judgment nor integrity & that he was unfitt to Judge in the Kings causes & that his manners were impertinent."

Lewis Morris was not a man who could ignore such an insult. The judge was known for his knowledge of the law. He was also a wily politician, always ready to fight his opponents.

In a letter to the governor, Morris wrote that judges should not give a legal opinion in order to please the governor or serve his personal interests. If judges did this, the people of New York would believe that the laws did not protect them.

"As to my Integrity," Morris continued indignantly, "I have been in this Office allmost Twenty Years, my Hands were never foul'd with a Bribe; . . . I have served the Publick faithfully and honestly, according to the best of my Knowledge."

Morris published his legal decision and his letter to Governor Cosby so that everyone in New York could read them. Many New Yorkers agreed with Judge Morris and even signed a testimonial to Morris's good work as a judge. People wanted their property protected by law. Without a jury to decide money and property disputes, colonists were afraid that the British or colonial governments might take away their property unfairly. When Cosby tried to use the courts for his own benefit, he seemed corrupt.

The Opinion and Argument of the Chief Justice of the Province of *New-York*, concerning the Jurisdiction of the supream Court of the said Province, *to determine Causes in a Course of Equity.*

The Second Editio Corrected and Amended.

To his Excellency *WILLIAM COSBY*, Esq; Captain, General, and Governour in Chief, of the Provinces of *New-York*, *New-Jersie*, and Territories thereon depending in *America*, *Vice* Admiral of the same, and Collonel in his Majesties Army, &c.

May it please Your Excellency ;

IN Obedience to your Commands, by Fredrick Moris Esq; deputy Secretary, to send you a Copy of what I read in the Supream Court, concerning its having a Jurisdiction to determine Causes in a Course of Equity, and, a second Message by him, to give it under my Hand, -- I send you not only what I read, but what I said on that Head, as far as I can charge my Memory ; what was said was spoken before a numerous Auditory, among which were the Grand Jury for the City and County of New-York, and several other Persons of Distinction. I have been told (but how truely I know not) that it has been represented to Your Excellency, that I would not suffer the King's Council to speak : If such an Account has been given you ? 'tis not true. Not only the Kings Council, but every Body else that had an Inclination to speak on that Head, had free Liberty to say what they thought proper, and a Gentleman that practised at the Bar adressed himself to the Court as an Amicus Curiæ, tho' he was then concern'd for his Client, to support the Jurisdiction of the Court in a Course of Equity, which at that Time was unknown to me. I choose this publick Method to prevent as much as I can any other Misrepresentation, and what I said is as follows, viz.

MY SON some Time since informed me, that in this Case of *Van Dam's* there was a Plea to the Jurisdiction of this Court, which I understood to be to its Jurisdiction of determining Matters in a Course of Equity ; upon which I took some Pains to inquire a litle into the Matter : But upon hearing the Plea I find it to be very different from what I understood it to be. And tho' from the Term *Plea* made use of, it seems contradictory ; because *ex vi termini*, a Plea

in

Judge Morris's Strike Against Governor Cosby *The first page of a pamphlet (second edition) that contains both Chief Justice Lewis Morris's written opinion in the Van Dam case and Morris's letter to Governor Cosby. Peter Zenger printed and sold the first edition of the fifteen-page pamphlet in April 1733. He later published the second edition to correct his numerous printing errors in the first one.*

Frustrated by Morris, Governor Cosby wrote to the Duke of Newcastle in London and listed his objections to Lewis Morris and his son Lewis Morris, Jr.: "It is evident from what has been said, that the Father on the Bench and the son in the Assembly act with the same views; they are men, from whom I am to expect the utmost opposition in the King's affairs and therefore ought to be crushed in time."

He went on to write: "I must either displace Morris or suffer myself to be affronted, or what is still worse, see the King's authority trampled on and disrespect and irreverence to it, taught, from the Bench to the People by him."

Cosby made the wrong choice. In August 1733, he stripped Morris of his judge-ship. It was a foolish move that shocked many New York colonists. Morris had held the position for eighteen years, and Cosby had acted without approval from the Provincial Council.

This was the spark that ignited a political fire. Judge Lewis Morris and Rip Van Dam had had enough of the new governor. They set out to destroy William Cosby. Joining them were four younger men: Van Dam's two lawyers, James Alexander and William Smith; Morris's son, Lewis Morris, Jr.; and a member of the Council, Cadwallader Colden. Their goal was to send William Cosby back to England.

WHO LIVED IN NEW YORK CITY?

In 1731, New York City had nearly nine thousand residents. The city was smaller than Philadelphia and Boston, but it had more types of people. Like today's New York, the colonial port city was a melting pot. It was home to people of many national backgrounds and languages: Dutch, English, French, German, Welsh, Swiss, and Scottish. About one in five was a black slave. New York residents were of several different religious faiths, including Anglican, Quaker, Dutch Reformed, Lutheran, Presbyterian, Baptist, Catholic, and Jewish.

APPRENTICES AND JOURNEYMEN

An owner of a printing shop needed workers to help him operate his business. He often used apprentices, training them in the craft of printing in exchange for their labor.

An apprentice usually began training with the master printer in his early teens. Peter Zenger was thirteen when he became William Bradford's apprentice. Some printers, including Bradford and Zenger, trained their own sons. But often the apprentice was not a relative of the printer. The master printer provided the apprentice's food, shelter, clothing, and perhaps some schooling. Over several years, the apprentice learned to set and ink the type and to operate the press.

By age twenty-one, the apprentice became a journeyman. Now he could move freely from job to job, working for whom he wanted and earning a wage. He could even set up his own printing shop if he had enough skill and the money to buy equipment.

Zenger's Arithmetic Book, 1730
Peter Zenger printed the first arithmetic textbook in the New York colony in 1730. This is the title page of the 124-page book of math problems, written in Dutch by Pieter Venema.

TWO

The *New-York Weekly Journal* Is Born
"We Extreamly want a good and nimble printer"

Governor Cosby paid no attention when people objected to his actions. After his advisors told him once that one of his ideas was against the law, Cosby was reported to have replied, "How, gentlemen, do you think I mind that, alas! I have a great interest in England."

By his interest in England, he meant his two powerful relatives, the Duke of Newcastle and the Earl of Halifax. These men had arranged Cosby's appointment as governor. They kept him out of trouble with the king.

The king intended his colonial governors to rule without stirring up public unrest. Lewis Morris, Rip Van Dam, and their friends planned to do plenty of stirring up. By turning public opinion against Cosby, they would get the governor in so much trouble that even his influential patrons couldn't help him.

At the same time, they hoped to gain support for their political party, nicknamed the Morrisites after Lewis Morris. Their opposition, the Court Party, supported Governor Cosby.

Autumn 1733: Finding a Printer

At first the Morrisites whipped up the public's anger with pamphlets detailing Governor Cosby's offensive actions. But they knew that they could reach more people if their criticisms were published in a newspaper. A newspaper would come out regularly and could cover more topics than a pamphlet.

Unlike today, when many cities have several newspapers, 1733 colonial New York had only one. It was the *New-York Gazette*, published by William Bradford. Bradford also happened to be the king's official printer. He would not print anything against

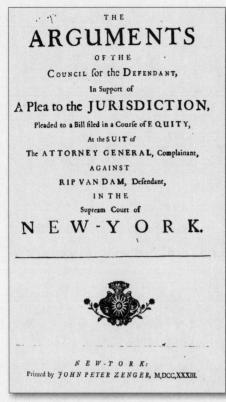

THE

ARGUMENTS

OF THE

COUNCIL for the DEFENDANT,

In Support of

A Plea to the JURISDICTION,

Pleaded to a Bill filed in a Courſe of E Q U I T Y,

At the S U I T of

The A T T O R N E Y G E N E R A L, Complainant,

AGAINST

RIP VAN DAM, Defendant,

IN THE

Supream Court of

N E W - Y O R K.

———————————————

N E W - Y O R K:
Printed by J O H N P E T E R Z E N G E R, M,DCC,XXXIII.

Zenger Pamphlet, 1733 *Peter Zenger had printed materials for the Morrisites before they asked him to print the* New-York Weekly Journal. *One example was this sixty-four-page pamphlet published in 1733. It contains the legal arguments presented by attorneys James Alexander and William Smith when they defended Rip Van Dam in the New York Supreme Court.*

JOHN PETER ZENGER
(1697–1746)

John Peter Zenger first saw New York City from the deck of a ship in 1710. The thirteen-year-old had sailed into the harbor from Europe with his widowed mother and younger brother and sister.

The family had traveled as part of a group of refugees called Palatines. The Palatines had left their homes in Germany to escape religious persecution and war. The British government arranged for more than two thousand of these Germans, including the Zengers, to settle in the New York colony.

Later that year, young Peter became an apprentice to New York's only printer, William Bradford. For the next eight years, the boy learned the trade of printing.

After finishing his apprenticeship, Peter moved to Maryland to set up his own printing business. He didn't stay long. His wife died, leaving him with a baby son. Zenger returned to New York City, where he married Anna Catharine Maulin, called Catharine, and joined William Bradford in business. He and Catharine had five children.

Zenger's partnership with Bradford lasted about a year. By 1726, he had opened his own printing shop in New York. As the second printer in the city, he had a modest business, printing mostly religious material such as sermons. Zenger printed the first arithmetic textbook in the New York colony.

When the Morrisites asked him to publish their newspaper in the fall of 1733, Peter Zenger's life changed forever.

the governor in the *Gazette* for fear of losing his well-paid position.

The *Gazette* praised Governor Cosby's actions. The flattering articles were written by Francis Harison, the governor's close advisor and strong ally on the Provincial Council.

The Morrisites had only one choice. They would have to start their own newspaper. Morrisite James Alexander wrote to his friend, the former New York governor Robert Hunter, who had become governor of Jamaica: "We Extreamly want a good and nimble printer which if we had he [Cosby] would Soon appear from the press in his proper Colours."

Where would they find a printer who owned a printing press? In the early 1700s, printing was a specialized skill. Few printers worked in the American colonies. Luckily for the Morrisites, New York had two.

Besides William Bradford, there was John Peter Zenger. Zenger was a thirty-six-year-old German immigrant who had been trained by Bradford. He had operated his printing shop on Smith Street in New York City for about seven years, publishing mostly religious material. Zenger had already printed pamphlets for the Morrisites. Earlier in the year, he had published Lewis Morris's letter to Governor Cosby after Cosby removed the Chief Justice from the Supreme Court. Peter Zenger was not as successful as Bradford. So when the Morrisites came to him, the struggling printer welcomed the business. Printing a newspaper would provide steady income for Zenger and his family.

THE VOICES BEHIND THE NEWSPAPER

The Morrisites did not need Peter Zenger to write their articles. His job was to set the type and print each edition of the newspaper.

James Alexander would be the editor and chief writer of the *New-York Weekly Journal*. Alexander was in his early forties. A well-educated man with piercing eyes, he was one of the most intelligent and talented lawyers in New York and New Jersey. Alexander was a member of both the New York and New Jersey Provincial Councils and was deeply involved in colonial politics.

Despite the demands of his law practice and large family of young children,

JAMES ALEXANDER
(1691–1756)

James Alexander was born in Scotland to an aristocratic family. He was educated in mathematics and served in the Royal Navy. After being involved in the Scottish opposition to the English king George I, Alexander had to flee to America in 1715.

Once in the colonies, Alexander studied law. His mathematics background helped him to think logically and to write forceful legal arguments. He was known as one of the most skillful attorneys in New York and New Jersey. Over the years, Alexander personally trained many young men who later became leading lawyers in the middle colonies.

Alexander married a wealthy widow with two young sons. She owned and continued to manage her late husband's store after her marriage to Alexander. They had seven more children together.

Alexander read widely and had a vast personal library. His knowledge of philosophy, law, and politics influenced the essays that he wrote in the *New-York Weekly Journal* about freedom and government. With Benjamin Franklin, Alexander helped start the American Philosophical Society. This group, still in existence, is dedicated to applying scientific knowledge to business and government.

The New-York Weekly Journal *Debuts with a Mistake* *Zenger printed the incorrect month in the nameplate of the* New-York Weekly Journal's *first issue: October 5, 1733. Later someone—perhaps a collector of colonial newspapers, historian, or librarian—made the notation: "Should be November." The* Journal *came out each Monday. "Munday" was the spelling used at the time. The stamp of the American Antiquarian Society in the upper right corner indicates that this organization owns the original copy of the first issue.*

Alexander eagerly took on the editorship of the *Journal*. He had a low opinion of Governor Cosby. To him, Cosby was a man who abused his power and took advantage of the colonists. He wrote to Robert Hunter: "Our Governour . . . has long agoe given more Distaste to the people here than I believe any Governour that ever this province had during his whole Government."

The governor didn't like the outspoken Alexander, either. Within months of Cosby's arrival in the province, he had written to London: "There is one James Alexander who I found here both in New York & Jerseys Councils, tho: very unfitt to sit in either, or indeed to act in any other capacity where His Majesty's honour and interest are concerned, he is the only man that has given me any uneasiness since my arrival."

Cosby wanted to replace Alexander on both Provincial Councils. When London did not respond to his request, the governor simply stopped sending notices of council meeting dates to Alexander and to the other Morrisites on the New York Council (Rip Van Dam, Cadwallader Colden, Philip Livingston, and Abraham Van Horne). Since just five council members were required to be present to carry on business, Cosby summoned only his supporters.

James Alexander was ready to take up the fight against the new governor. He, his law partner William Smith, and Lewis Morris would write most of the *Journal's* articles attacking Cosby. Cadwallader Colden and Lewis Morris, Jr., probably wrote some material, too.

The men did not sign their real names or reveal that they were behind the newspaper. They knew that they could be arrested for criticizing the government in print. Peter Zenger must have known it, too, but he was willing to take the risk.

NOVEMBER 1733: THE *New-York Weekly Journal* DEBUTS

The *Journal's* first issue appeared on Monday, November 5, 1733. Zenger printed the date as October 5, 1733, a sign of his carelessness.

The newspaper contained four pages, each about the size of a sheet of notebook paper. The *Journal* announced that it was "Printed and Sold by John Peter Zenger: By whom Subscriptions for this Paper are taken in, at Three Shillings per Quarter."

NEW YORK : Printed and Sold by *John Peter Zenger* : By whom Subscriptions for this Paper are taken in, at Three Shillings *per* Quarter.

Worth Every Shilling! *At the bottom of the Journal's last page, Zenger printed the newspaper's price. The Morrisites didn't start the Journal to make money. Their goal was to use the newspaper to influence New York politics.*

New York's Quakers *Quakers gather under the oak trees in Flushing (Long Island), New York, in 1672. Quakers settled in New York in the 1650s while the Dutch still controlled the colony. In the 1733 New York Assembly elections, the Quakers supported Lewis Morris, but Cosby's supporters wouldn't let them vote. The painting, by French artist Jacques Gerard Milbert (1766–1840), was created around 1825 to show the visit of George Fox, the founder of the Quaker religion in England.*

In today's money, the weekly paper cost readers about $13 for three months, which was not too expensive. Subscribers shared copies of the newspaper with friends. The *Journal* was also read aloud in taverns and other gathering places. Probably about half of New Yorkers couldn't read. These people had no formal schooling or were immigrants who did not speak English well.

The *Journal*'s nameplate announced that the newspaper would contain "the freshest Advices, Foreign, and Domestick." Indeed, the first issue printed foreign news from Europe on page 2. It was not actually "fresh." The events had happened three or four months earlier and were copied from European newspapers.

On the other hand, the domestic, or local, news *was* fresh. On pages 3 and 4, the *Journal* reported on the Assembly election held the week before. In the election, Lewis Morris ran for assemblyman from Westchester County, near New York City.

The *Journal* accused Governor Cosby and the Court Party of rigging the election against Morris. An article explained that the sheriff, who had been appointed by Cosby, had illegally prevented thirty-eight Quakers from voting. It was well known that the Quakers supported Lewis Morris.

The sheriff said the Quakers were ineligible to vote because they refused to swear that they were qualified voters. Quakers believed that the Bible forbade them from taking such an oath. In past elections, however, sheriffs had allowed Quakers to vote anyway. The *Journal* charged that the sheriff's action was "contrary to Law, and a violent Attempt of the Liberties of the People."

Lewis Morris won the election in a landslide even without the Quaker vote. The *Journal* made sure that the public knew how Cosby's friends had treated the Quakers. The news article repeatedly referred to the popular judge as the "late Chief Justice." This reminded readers that Governor Cosby had fired Morris from the Supreme Court.

James Alexander sent a copy of the *Journal*'s first issue to Robert Hunter. He added a note: "Inclosed is also the first of a News paper designed to be Continued Weekly, & Chiefly to Expose him [Governor Cosby] & those ridiculous flatteries with which Mr. Harrison [Francis Harison, Cosby's ally who wrote for the *Gazette*] loads our other News paper."

PRINTING THE *NEW-YORK WEEKLY JOURNAL*

Each week editor James Alexander handed Peter Zenger material to include in the *Journal*. To print it, Zenger copied the words and sentences using metal letters. He picked up the letters by hand, one at a time, and slid the type onto a composing stick. The letters had to be placed upside down and backward. It was a difficult task.

Next the printer gathered the lines of type together and locked them into a metal frame that held two pages of type. It could take several hours just to set the type for one page.

The printer locked the frame of letters onto the wooden printing press. Another workman usually had the job of spreading ink over the metal letters with a leather ball. Paper made from cloth rags was put into the printing press. A worker pulled a handle that pressed the paper sheet onto the inked type.

Each sheet had to be fed through the press individually. If the men were working fast, the press could print about two hundred sheets in an hour.

After the *Journal* was printed on both sides of the sheet, the damp paper was hung up until it was dry. Then it was folded once to form two leaves, or four pages. Finally the newspaper was ready to hand out to customers.

Because a printer needed good light to see what he was doing, he had to do most of his work during daylight hours. Printing each issue of the *Journal* probably took Zenger several days.

Working the Press *Workers in a typical printing shop of Zenger's time. This early twentieth-century painting,* Franklin, the Printer *by Charles E. Mills, shows a young Benjamin Franklin at his printing press in Philadelphia during the same period that Peter Zenger was printing the* New-York Weekly Journal *in New York.*

The *Journal* grabbed the attention of New Yorkers. Some of the early issues sold out and had to be reprinted to satisfy reader demand. That was exactly what the Morrisites had hoped for. People were reading their newspaper.

SEDITIOUS LIBEL

The English law against seditious libel applied to the American colonies. A person charged with seditious libel was accused of printing criticisms of the government or its officials. Leaders were afraid that such insults would weaken them and make it hard for them to govern. Furthermore, the criticism might stir up rebellion.

The punishment for seditious libel was prison, fines, or sometimes both. The government could burn printed material and take the printer's press.

It did not matter whether the criticisms were true or false. In fact, the libel was considered more serious if the published statements were true. Then people would believe the charges and have less confidence in the government.

For example, in its December 17, 1733, issue, the *New-York Weekly Journal* accused Governor Cosby of threatening New York's security when he foolishly allowed a French boat to enter the harbor. Suppose it were true that Cosby had intentionally cooperated with a British enemy, knowing that the French were scouting the harbor for a future attack. The people of New York would believe that the governor was a traitor. This would make it impossible for Cosby to govern.

During a trial, the jury was only allowed to decide whether the accused person had actually published the words. The judges decided whether the words had criticized the government.

FRANCE, THE COLONIAL ENEMY

England and France fought four wars from 1689 to 1763 over control of North America. Both countries worked to establish alliances with the Indian tribes. During this period, France controlled most of present-day Canada and areas west of New York. The New York colonists worried that the French and their Indian allies would attack and take over New York lands. The colonists weren't confident that the British government would protect them.

THREE

The *Journal* on the Attack
"A Monkey . . . has lately broke his Chain"

WINTER 1733–1734: ESSAYS ABOUT FREEDOM

Every week the shop on Smith Street bustled as Peter Zenger printed the *New-York Weekly Journal*. With the help of his journeyman and his sons, Zenger set the type, printed the pages, and hung the paper sheets until the black ink dried. Each Monday New York readers awaited the latest attack on Governor Cosby.

Cosby gave the *Journal* plenty to criticize. Again and again, he used his power to take advantage of New Yorkers. He demanded money from people in exchange for government jobs. He obtained land for himself and his friends. The Morrisites accused Cosby of personally using money that had been sent from London for soldier pay and for gifts to the Iroquois Indians, who were allies of the British. When the Morrisites gained strength in the Assembly after the 1733 elections, the governor improperly halted the Assembly's meetings for six months.

The *Journal* reported on all of it. Sometimes editor James Alexander used a news article to detail Cosby's misdeeds. In other cases, a letter to the newspaper outlined the abuse. Most letters were either unsigned or signed with false names. This protected the authors—usually the Morrisites—from being identified and later charged with seditious libel for criticizing Cosby and his administration.

James Alexander also included essays declaring that citizens should have more power and rights. Some essays were written by English authors. They had been published earlier in England, and Zenger reprinted them in the *Journal*. Alexander and other Morrisites wrote original essays, too, never signing their real names.

Many essays argued that a free press was needed to expose corrupt governments. An anonymous essay printed in the *Journal*'s second and third issues said that

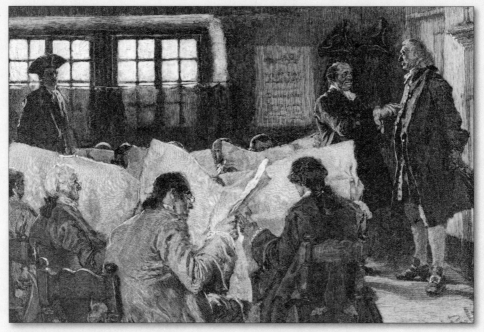

The Newspaper Reaches Its Readers Colonial newspapers reached many more people than the paid subscribers. During the 1700s, newspapers were read aloud in gathering places such as coffeehouses and taverns, as shown in this Howard Pyle illustration from 1890. Pyle (1853–1911), who was known for the historical detail of his work, illustrated many popular books and magazines.

ADVERTISEMENT.

A Large Spaneil, of about Five Foot Five Inches High, has lately ſtray'd from his Kennell with his Mouth full of fulſom Panegericks, and in his Ramble dropt them in the NEW-YORK-GAZETTE; when a Puppy, he was mank'd thus Ⅎ Ⅱ, and a Croſs in his Forehead, but the Mark being worn out, he has taken upon him in an heatheniſh Manner to abuſe Mankind, by impoſing a great many groſs Falſhoods upon them. Whoever will ſtrip the ſaid Panagericks of all their Fulſomneſs, and ſend the Beaſt back to his Kennell, ſhall have the Thanks of all honeſt Men, and all reaſonable Charges.

Harison Is a Dog The Journal pokes fun at Francis Harison, a Cosby supporter, by comparing him to a dog in the November 26, 1733, issue.

ADVERTISEMENTS.

A Monkey of the larger Sort, about four Foot high, has lately broke his Chain, and run into the Country, where he has play'd many a Monkey Trick: Amongſt the reſt, he having by ſome Means or other got a Warr Saddle, Piſtols and Sword, this Whimſical Creature fancied himſelf a General; and taking a Paper in his Paw he muttered over it, what the far greateſt Part of the Company underſtood not: but others who thought themſelves wiſer pretended to underſtand him; at their Motion a numerous Company preſent divided: And tho' there was a conſiderable Majority on one Side, yet Pug was not ſatisfied, but by Grimace and Chattering ſhew'd a great Uneaſineſs. In order to ſatisfy him, (as by his Appearance he was judged to belong to ſome Perſon of Quality) the Company repaired to a Houſe at ſome ſmall Diſtance, where every Man's Name was called over and written down; but a Man ap-

. . . And Cosby Is a Monkey In this mock advertisement from the December 10, 1733, New-York Weekly Journal, Governor Cosby is compared to a monkey.

people must have the freedom to express opinions. Without it, they were no more than slaves: "No Nation Antient or Modern ever lost the Liberty of freely Speaking, Writing, or Publishing their Sentiments, but forthwith lost their Liberty in general and became Slaves."

Poking Fun

Editor Alexander made sure that the *Journal* contained humor to entertain the readers. He made up advertisements and slipped them into the paid advertising section along with notices about house sales and runaway apprentices. Much like political cartoons in modern newspapers, these ads poked fun at Cosby and his supporters.

One example compared Governor Cosby to a monkey who plays tricks on the people of New York: "A Monkey of the larger Sort . . . has lately broke his Chain, and run into the Country, where he has playd many a Monkey Trick. . . . Whosoever shall take this little mischievous Animal, and send him back to his Master, so that he may be chained up again, shall have for his Reward a Thousand Thanks."

Another humorous advertisement mocked Francis Harison, a Cosby supporter on the Provincial Council: "A Large Spaneil, of about Five Foot Five Inches High, has lately stray'd from his Kennell . . . he has taken upon him . . . to abuse Mankind, by imposing a great many gross Falshoods upon them. Whoever will . . . send the Beast back to his Kennell, shall have the Thanks of all honest Men."

A Paper War

By December 1733, Governor Cosby could take no more. He complained in a letter to the Duke of Newcastle that the Morrisites were trying "to provoke me to enter into a paper warr to justifye the proceedings of the Court, my owne conduct, and his Majesty's authority." Cosby feared that a battle between newspapers would turn the public against him.

A paper war is exactly what happened. Cosby told William Bradford to publish responses to the *Journal*'s attacks in the *New-York Gazette*. Francis Harison wrote most of these. Now New Yorkers could read the bitter verbal daggers thrown by both sides.

KLAGTE
Van Eenige Leeden der
NEDERDUYTSE HERVORMDE KE
Woonende op *Raretans, &c.* in de Provincie van
NIEU-JERSEY, in *NOORD-AMERICA,*
Onder de Kroon van *Groot-Brittanje.*
Over het GEDRAG, Aldaar en Elders,
Abraham VAN *Gatej*
Do. *THEODORUS JACOBUS FRILINGHUISEN,*
Met syn Kerken-Raaden.
TEN
ANTWOORD
Op hunne
Ban-Dreygende Daag-Brieven, &c.
AAN
Alle *Liefhebbers der Waarheyd,* ter onderfoek, voorgefteld,
Hoe Die Gegrond zyn, of Niet.
Abraham ET een *Gatej*
Noodige Voor-Reeden, tot opheldering van de *Klagte.*
Uytgegeven Door
De Gevolmagtigden der gemelde Leeden.

Te New-York, Gedrukt by William Bradford en J. Peter Zenger. 1725.

The Zenger-Bradford Partnership *The title page of a Dutch religious pamphlet printed by Peter Zenger and William Bradford in 1725 when they worked as partners. It is the only known printed document on which both names appear.*

WILLIAM BRADFORD
(1663–1752)

Some historians call William Bradford "the father of American printing" because he established the first printing press in two colonies—Pennsylvania and New York. He was "the father" literally, too, because his son, grandson, and great-grandson became famous colonial printers.

Born in England, Bradford learned the printing business in London. He immigrated to Pennsylvania when he was about twenty years old and set up a printing press in Philadelphia. In 1693, he moved to New York, where he became the official printer, a post he held for fifty years. Bradford started the *New-York Gazette* in 1725, continuing the newspaper until he retired in 1744.

WHAT IS A GRAND JURY?

In New York in the 1730s, a grand jury was made up of nineteen men. Their names were picked from a list of property owners. A new grand jury was chosen twice a year.

The grand jury's job was to decide whether it appeared that a crime had been committed and if the accused person might have done it. The grand jury came to its decision after listening to evidence presented by the government's lawyer, called the attorney general.

If the grand jury thought there was enough evidence, it indicted, or charged, the person with the crime. Then the accused person went to trial. At the trial, a different jury decided whether he or she was guilty of the crime, or if there had even been a crime.

If the grand jury did not indict, the person was freed and no trial occurred.

The *Gazette* joined the name-calling by giving nicknames to the Morrisites. Their true identities were well known to readers. Wild Peter from the Banks of the Rhine was German immigrant Peter Zenger (the Rhine is a river in Germany). The Amsterdam Crane was Rip Van Dam, who had Dutch ancestors (Amsterdam is a Dutch city).

Using strong language, the *Gazette* accused Zenger of printing spiteful lies: "I fear if he [Zenger] goes on at this Rate, he will print himself into a Proverb, and when any thing false and scandalous is publickly Reported, it will be call'd A ZENGER."

The *Journal* shot back that because of Cosby's abuses, "the Enjoyment of the Lives, Liberties, and Estates of the Inhabitants are thereby rendered Precarious and Uncertain."

To that, the *Gazette* responded that the *Journal* had used lies to turn the public against Cosby's government: "'Tis not difficult to inflame a Nation, and we have frequent Instances in Story of Men who had nothing but the Appearances of Worth, with false Vertue, false Parts, and false Eloquence, who yet became so popular that they were able to disturb their Country's Peace."

COSBY USES THE COURTS

As the criticisms of him continued, Governor Cosby became determined to silence the *Journal*. He decided to use the courts to do this. Cosby had influence within the legal system. After firing Lewis Morris as chief justice of the Supreme Court, the governor had appointed James De Lancey to the position. De Lancey was one of Cosby's supporters on the Provincial Council.

On a cold January day in 1733/34, Judge De Lancey addressed a grand jury of nineteen men in the courtroom of City Hall. He asked the jury to hand down indictments, or charges, against the libels that had been appearing in the *Journal* since November:

"Some Men . . . have spread abroad many seditious Libels, in order to lessen in the People's Minds the Regard which is due to a Person in his [the governor's] high Station."

Cadwallader Colden (1688–1776), a Scotsman, trained as a doctor in London and immigrated to America in 1710. Colden was a leading scientist of his day, as well as a politician. During his career, he served in the New York Provincial Council and as acting governor.

To my Subscribers and Wellwishers;

NOw when Forreign News is not to be had, and all other News Writers in these Countries are at a Loss how to continue their Papers, and what to fill them up with; I must acknowledge my Obligations to you to be such, that you do so plentifully supply me, that tho' for some Weeks past I have used my smallest Letter, and to put as much into a Paper as was in my Power, yet I have now Supplies sufficient to fill above seven weekly Papers more. This I mention that my Correspondents whose Works have not presently a Place in my Journal may know the Cause of it and excuse it for a Time, assuring them, that Justice shall be done to their Labours as soon as I possibly can, at least so much of them as I am advised I dare safely print, and in order to do Justice to every one, I have thought of publishing a Thursdays Journal weekly for the next Quarter, if my Subscribers for this Mondays Journal, will on their first Quarters Payment signify their desire of it either by Letter or Subscription for that Purpose on the like Terms with this Paper, which I beg they'll consider of and signify their Inclinations, and if a sufficient Number to bear the Charge, approve of it, it shall (God willing) be done.

I am
your obliged humble Servant,
J. Peter Zenger.

It's a Hit A notice in the January 21, 1733/34, issue hints that the Journal was a hit with readers. Zenger considered adding an extra edition on Thursdays because the newspaper had been receiving more letters to the editor than he could fit in the Monday edition. But subscribers must not have been willing to pay for an extra issue each week; the Journal continued as only a once-a-week newspaper.

The Printer hereof intends to remove to Broad-Street near the upper End of the Long Bridge,

A New Shop for Zenger In the Journal's May 6, 1734, issue, Zenger announced that he was moving his printing shop to Broad Street, apparently a better location.

De Lancey added: "The Authors are not certainly known, and yet it is an easy Matter to guess who they are."

The jurors undoubtedly knew who the authors were. It was no secret to most New Yorkers that the Morrisites were behind the *Journal* and that Peter Zenger was its printer and publisher. Yet the jurors did not cooperate with Governor Cosby and Judge De Lancey. They refused to indict anyone for seditious libel, saying that there wasn't enough evidence for a trial.

In writing about the Zenger case later, Cadwallader Colden reported that Cosby "was very generally disliked & for that reason the papers [the *New-York Weekly Journal*] were as generally approved of [and] it would not be easy to find a Grand Jury in New York to find an Indictment upon them." The *Journal* would continue.

SPRING 1734: TEMPERS RUN HIGH

The back and forth between the *Journal* and *Gazette* was good for business. The *Journal* sold well enough for Zenger to move his printing shop to a more central location on Broad Street.

As business boomed, tempers ran high. James Alexander claimed that Francis Harison wrote him an anonymous letter threatening to poison his family. Governor Cosby's wife told friends that it was her highest wish to see Alexander and William Smith hanged at the gallows in front of the fort's gate.

The *Gazette* claimed that Zenger's newspaper was nothing but "infamous, agravated Libels, virulent, dull." The *Journal* replied that at least "the People of this Province as yet enjoy the Benefit of the Liberty of the Presse."

But even Morrisite Cadwallader Colden later admitted that the *Journal* might have gone too far with its attacks: "The Writers in that paper exposed the Actions of Governor's party in the worst light they could place them & among other well wrote papers published several that could not be justified & of which perhaps the Authors upon more cool reflexion are now ashamed for in some of them they raked into mens private Weaknesses & secrets of Families which had no Relation to the publick."

The war of words between the Morrisites and Cosby supporters went on through the spring and summer of 1734. It was about to turn more serious.

The Journal *Gets New Yorkers Talking* The Journal's criticisms of
Governor Cosby became a topic of conversation for New York citizens.
This 1893 illustration by Howard Pyle shows people meeting and
talking along the New York waterfront during the eighteenth century.
New York was a major colonial port.

FOUR

The Governor Fights Back

"Inflaming their Minds,. . . disturbing the Peace"

SUMMER AND EARLY FALL 1734: FALSE AND SCANDALOUS LIBELS

The *Journal*'s nameplate promised the "freshest advices" every week. For Governor William Cosby, each week brought "fresh" attacks and insults. He knew that people were talking about him in the taverns and on the streets. Thanks to the *Journal*, his authority as governor was threatened. Cosby wished the Morrisites would disappear from his life.

In June, Governor Cosby sent a letter to the Board of Trade in London. He complained bitterly about the Morrisites, whose "open and implacable malice against me has appeared weekly in false and scandalous libels printed in Zengers Journal."

Cosby was right to think that the *Journal* had turned the public against him. That was proved at the end of September 1734. In the New York City Common Council election, the Morrisite Party defeated Cosby's Court Party allies in a landslide victory.

The Morrisites boasted of their win, which irritated Governor Cosby even more. Soon sheets of humorous songs about the election appeared on the streets. The songs made fun of Cosby and his Court Party supporters.

One verse referred to the way the governor removed Lewis Morris as supreme court chief justice and replaced him with Cosby ally James De Lancey:

> *"Tho' pettyfogging knaves deny*
> *us Rights of Englishmen;*
> *We'll make the scoundrel rascals fly,*
> *and ne'er return again.*
> *Our Judges they would chop and change*

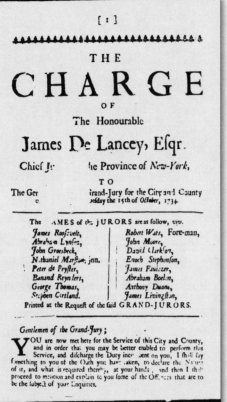

The Government Tries Again to Indict Zenger
The first page of Judge De Lancey's charge to the grand jury on October 15, 1734. William Bradford printed and sold the eight-page document. In his charge, De Lancey urged the jurors to indict Zenger for seditious libel as the printer of the insulting songs. The jury refused.

"Pettyfogging Knaves" *This one-sheet broadside includes the two songs written by the Morrisites and printed by Peter Zenger in 1734. The verses made fun of Governor Cosby and his Court Party supporters.*

for those that serve their turn,
And will not surely think it strange
if they for this should mourn."

The people of New York City had a good laugh over the songs. Cosby was not amused. Although the songs were unsigned, the governor was sure that Peter Zenger had printed them. Who else could have? The only other printer in New York was William Bradford. Cosby knew that Bradford would never print such slurs against him.

October 1734: "Put a Stop to Them"

Cosby was furious. The governor instructed Judge James De Lancey to urge a second grand jury to indict Peter Zenger. The charge: seditious libel for printing the insulting songs.

As he had in January, Judge De Lancey did his best. He tried to convince jurors that indicting Zenger was the only way to stop the public unrest stirred up by the Morrisites.

"It is high time to put a stop to them [libels]," De Lancey said in the courtroom, "for at the Rate things are now carried on . . . must not these things end in *Sedition*, if not timely prevented? . . . If you, *Gentlemen*, do not interpose, consider whether the ill Consequences that may arise from any Disturbances of the *Publick Peace*, may not, in part, lye at your door?"

The grand jury was not swayed by Judge De Lancey's appeal. The nineteen grand jurors reported that they could find no evidence to identify the author, printer, or publisher of the songs. They refused to indict Zenger.

November 1734: The Burning

Failing with the grand jury, Cosby went to the Provincial Council. He persuaded its members to ask the Assembly to join with the Council in ordering the public burning of four issues of the *Journal* from December 1733, September 1734, and October 1734.

In those issues, the *Journal* had accused Cosby of acting against the king's

The French Threat *French soldiers and their Indian allies in a 1757 battle against British soldiers and colonists. France and England fought for control of North America from 1689 to 1763. This late nineteenth-century engraving by Alfred Bobbett (1824–1888 or 1889) was based on the artwork of Felix Octavius Carr Darley (1822–1888), a famous illustrator of American books and magazines.*

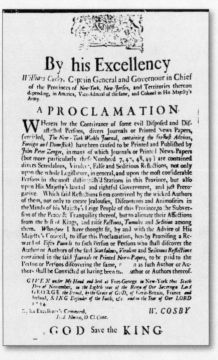

Reward! *In a proclamation on November 6, 1734, Governor Cosby promised £50 reward for the name of the authors of the New-York Weekly Journal. Cosby called these authors "evil Disposed and Disaffected Persons." William Bradford printed the one-page sheet. The design on the top is the royal seal of Great Britain.*

instructions in dealing with the Assembly and Provincial Council. It also had accused the governor of allowing a French boat into New York Harbor. This, the *Journal* said, gave the French the opportunity to "view their [New York's] Fortifications, sound their Harbours, tarry in their Country to discover their Strength." Since the English and French were enemies, the *Journal* came close to calling Cosby a traitor.

The Assembly would not order the newspapers burned. The elected officials knew that the public disapproved of Cosby's actions against Zenger.

Likewise, New York City's leaders refused to direct the burning as ordered by the Provincial Council. They announced that they would have nothing to do with the matter "since an Assembly of the Province, and several Grand Juries, have refused to meddle with the Papers."

Because the Assembly and city would not cooperate, the sheriff and several other Cosby supporters had to carry out the Council's order themselves. At noon on Wednesday, November 6, they gathered on the street in front of City Hall. One of the men built a fire on the cobblestones. Then the sheriff told his slave to throw the copies of the *Journal* onto the fire. As the black man tossed the newspapers into the flames, the paper sheets crackled and burned to ash.

An Order Is Issued

Governor Cosby didn't seem to understand that New Yorkers disapproved of what he was doing to Peter Zenger. Or perhaps he didn't care what they thought. In any case, he doggedly pushed toward his goal of shutting down the *Journal*.

On the day of the burning, Governor Cosby issued a proclamation. It promised £50 reward to anyone who could identify the authors of the seditious libels printed in the *Journal*. Another £20 was offered for the authors of the songs.

The reward was a large sum (about $4,200 and $1,700 in today's money). Everyone knew that James Alexander and other Morrisites had written the material. Yet no one claimed the reward. Governor Cosby did not obtain the proof he needed to arrest the authors and silence them for good.

No matter, thought Cosby. He could still shut down the *Journal* by arresting the

NEW-YORK : Printed and Sold by *John Peter Zenger* : By whom Subfcriptions for this Paper are taken at three Shillings *per* Quarter ; and Advertifements at three Shillings the firft Week, and one Shilling every Week after.

Zenger's Name on the Line *Every issue of the New-York Weekly Journal identified John Peter Zenger at the bottom of the fourth page. As printer and publisher, Zenger was legally responsible for the newspaper's content, even if he didn't write it himself. This comes from the October 28, 1734, issue.*

The Journal *Burns* *The burning of the New-York Weekly Journal on November 6, 1734, in front of City Hall. The cage, pillory, and stocks were used to punish certain lawbreakers by exposing them to public scorn. The church at the far end of the street is Trinity Church, where James Alexander and William Bradford were later buried. This 1908 illustration by artist Harry Fenn is based on historical records and drawings.*

printer. Zenger identified himself in every issue of the newspaper: "Printed and Sold by John Peter Zenger." As printer and publisher, the German immigrant was legally responsible for the newspaper's content even if he hadn't written it.

Once the Morrisites' printer was found guilty of seditious libel in court—and Cosby was confident that he would be—the governor's opponents would no longer be able to publish their newspaper.

As Cosby wanted, the Provincial Council ordered Zenger's arrest:

"It is ordered that the Sheriff for the City of *New-York,* do forthwith take and apprehend *John Peter Zenger,* for printing and publishing several Seditious Libels, dispersed throughout his Journals or News Papers, entitled *The New-York Weekly Journal* . . . as having in them many Things, tending to raise Factions and Tumults, among the People of this Province, inflaming their Minds with Contempt of His Majesty's Government, and greatly disturbing the Peace thereof, and upon his taking the said *John Peter Zenger, to commit him to the Prison or common Goal of the said City and County.*"

On Sunday, November 17, 1734, the sheriff carried out the Council's order. He arrested Peter Zenger in his shop on Broad Street as the printer prepared the *Journal* for publication the next day.

WILLIAM SMITH
(1697–1769)

At age seventeen, William Smith emigrated from England to New York with his family. On the ship crossing the Atlantic Ocean, he met his future law partner, twenty-four-year-old James Alexander. Alexander was on his way to a new home, too. The two were perfect partners. Smith was a fiery, rousing speaker. Alexander wrote brilliant legal arguments.

William Smith had a distinguished career as an attorney, judge, and politician. In 1732 he helped establish the first public school in New York.

Smith and his wife had fifteen children. Their oldest son, William Smith, Jr. (1728–1793), later wrote a history of the Province of New York that detailed events leading up to the Zenger trial.

FIVE

Imprisoned

"I had not the Liberty of Pen, Ink, or Paper"

NOVEMBER 1734: IN THE ATTIC JAIL

Peter Zenger was taken a few blocks from his printing shop to City Hall. There he was locked in the third-floor jail. The weather in mid-November had the bite of winter. Gaps in the low, sloping wooden ceiling let in cold drafts. For more than two days Zenger was not allowed to see or talk to anyone. He was miserable.

The arrest angered and worried New Yorkers. What authority did Governor Cosby have to imprison the printer? Two grand juries had found no reason to charge Zenger with seditious libel. The Assembly and city government would have nothing to do with the case. New Yorkers did not like the governor abusing his power to have a citizen thrown in jail.

Finally, six days after his arrest, Zenger appeared in court with his lawyers, James Alexander and William Smith. Spectators crowded the courtroom to show their support for the printer.

Alexander and Smith asked that bail be set so that Zenger could leave jail. Judge James De Lancey set bail at £400. This was equal to about $34,000 in today's money. Until Zenger paid it, he would remain behind bars.

Alexander and Smith protested, saying that such a high amount was against the intention of English law. They argued to Judge De Lancey that "excessive bail ought not to be required."

Peter Zenger told the judge, "I [am] not worth forty pounds (the tools of my trade and wearing apparel excepted)." The bail is "ten times more than [is] in my power" to pay.

Judge De Lancey did not change his mind. Peter Zenger was taken back to his jail cell in the City Hall attic above the courtroom.

"I Was Put Under Such Restraint" The Morrisites used Zenger's imprisonment to stoke the public's outrage over Governor Cosby's actions. Page 1 of the Journal's November 25, 1734, issue (shown here) describes Zenger's arrest and jailing the week before. The second column contains an essay about liberty of the press written in the form of a letter.

The Morrisites chose not to pay the printer's bail, although they could have collected the money. Perhaps they thought that if Zenger were released from jail, Cosby would arrest one or more of their group for writing the articles in the *Journal*. They knew that even higher bails might be set for them.

Besides, they didn't think that Peter Zenger would have to stay in jail long. Two grand juries had found nothing against him. Cosby could hold the printer for no more than a few weeks, until the third grand jury finished its work. No one expected this grand jury to indict Zenger, either. Meanwhile, the Morrisites would use Zenger's imprisonment to their political advantage by tapping into the public's outrage about it.

THE *Journal* CONTINUES

Governor Cosby had assumed that by jailing Zenger, he would silence the Morrisites. Without a printer, they could no longer publish the *Journal*.

Indeed, the newspaper did not appear as usual the next day. To Cosby's alarm, however, this was the only week that the *Journal* failed to reach its readers. It was published throughout the printer's imprisonment, most likely by editor James Alexander working with Zenger's journeyman and family.

In future issues, the Morrisites played to their readers' sympathy for the printer. For example, on the following Monday, November 25, the *Journal*'s front page reported the details of his jailing in a letter signed "J. Peter Zenger." James Alexander was probably the ghostwriter.

"To all my Subscribers and Benefactors who take my weekly Journall. . . . I was put under such Restraint that I had not the Liberty of Pen, Ink, or Paper, or to see, or speak with People, till . . . the *Wednesday* following. . . . I have had since that Time, the Liberty of Speaking through the Hole of the Door, to my Wife and Servants . . . I hope for the future by the Liberty of Speaking to my Servants thro' the Hole of the Door of the Prison, to entertain you with my weekly *Journal* as formerly."

The rest of the front page was a letter to the editor praising the importance of a free press. Alexander probably wrote that, too, because it repeated his ideas about freedom from government control. To emphasize the point, the word *Liberty* was used eight times on the front page.

THE MYTH ABOUT ZENGER'S WIFE

Over the years, stories have appeared about Catharine Zenger's role in printing and publishing the *Journal*. Some accounts claim that she created the newspaper and wrote the contents. Others say that Catharine single-handedly printed the *Journal* during her husband's imprisonment. These are myths.

The only thing known for sure about Catharine is that her name was listed as publisher of the *Journal* and other printed material, such as almanacs, for two years following Peter Zenger's death. At the end of two years, she turned the printing business over to her stepson, John Zenger.

Historical evidence proves that James Alexander and other Morrisites started the *Journal* and were the authors of essays and articles in the newspaper. No evidence exists that Catharine or Peter wrote any of the essays or that they had the education to do so.

During colonial times, it was not uncommon for a printer's wife to manage a printing shop after her husband died. Catharine might have helped to run the business while Zenger was alive, too. But there is no evidence that she was trained as a printer. It is likely that Zenger's journeyman and his sons, who had been trained by their father, did the actual printing while Zenger was in jail. During the printer's trial, the attorney general had planned to call them as witnesses to testify about the printing of the *Journal*.

NEW-YORK: *Printed by the Widow* Cathrine Zenger, *where Advertisements are taken in.*

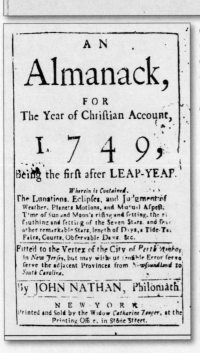

Catharine Zenger Takes Over the Journal In the October 13, 1746, issue of the Journal, *Catharine Zenger announced that she was taking over her husband's business and the printing of the newspaper. In this issue, Catharine printed her name without the second a, probably by mistake.*

Almanac Printed by Catharine Zenger *Catharine Zenger printed and sold a 1749 almanac, written by John Nathan. The annual almanac was important to colonists. It contained such useful information as weather predictions, a planting calendar, and court session dates.*

December 1734: "From My Prison"

Later, letters titled "From my Prison" appeared in the newspaper, supposedly written by Peter Zenger. James Alexander was likely the author. The writing contained Latin phrases and references to law and philosophy, which Zenger, who lacked Alexander's formal education, probably would not have known.

The *Journal* reminded readers that Zenger had been treated without regard to law. One letter dated December 20, 1734, told readers how Zenger had been abused upon his arrest: "Alterations were purposely Made on my Account, to put me into a Place by myself, where I was so strictly confin'd above 50 Hours that my Wife might not speak to me but in presence of the Subsherrif."

Although the Morrisites were successful in rousing public anger over Zenger's jailing, they realized that the arrest signaled serious problems ahead. They had spent a year relentlessly criticizing Governor Cosby. Yet they had failed to get him removed from office by British officials. Now Cosby's actions had become more threatening. It was time to do more.

Lewis Morris decided to travel to England to meet face-to-face with British officials in charge of colonial matters. James Alexander wrote a list of demands for Morris to present to them. Besides removal of Cosby, the list included reinstating Morris as supreme court chief justice.

The *Journal* reported that Lewis Morris sailed for London the Saturday after Zenger's arrest. He would discuss "Matters of great Importance at the Court of Great Brittain." While Morris took the case against Cosby to London, Alexander and the other Morrisites continued their printed attacks every Monday in the *Journal*.

CITY HALL

Peter Zenger was jailed and tried in City Hall on Wall Street in New York City. The three-story brick building was erected around 1700. It was the home of the city's Common Council, the city court, the New York Supreme Court, and the Provincial Assembly. The Provincial Council met at Fort George.

WILLIAM BRADFORD'S TRIAL

More than thirty years before Zenger's arrest, William Bradford was arrested in Pennsylvania on the same charge.

In 1692, Bradford printed writings critical of the Quaker leaders who ran Philadelphia. For this, he was charged with "Publishing, Uttering and Spreading a Malitious and Seditious paper" that undermined the government. Bradford and others involved in the criticism were jailed.

During his trial, Bradford argued that his pamphlet was not seditious. When the jury could not decide whether he had actually printed the writings, Bradford was released from jail.

Because he had gotten on the wrong side of Pennsylvania's Quaker leaders, Bradford decided to move to New York. In 1693, he became the province's official royal printer.

Eighteenth-Century Printing Press
Peter Zenger and William Bradford used a printing press like this one to print their newspapers.

SIX

Hope Fades

"False, malicious, seditious [and] scandalous"

As the cold winds of winter gripped New York, the battle between the Morrisites and Governor Cosby heated up. With Lewis Morris in London, James Alexander led the attack against Cosby in New York on the pages of the *Journal*.

Meanwhile, Peter Zenger sat in his jail cell on the third floor of City Hall. He knew that James Alexander and William Smith were the best lawyers in New York. But what if they were wrong about his being released soon? How long could his printing business survive in his absence? How would his wife and six children eat if Governor Cosby found a way to close down the press?

Finally the day came that Zenger had been awaiting since November. At the end of January, the attorney general, at Governor Cosby's urging, asked a grand jury to indict Zenger. Once again, the grand jury—the third one—found nothing against the printer. Without an indictment to hold him in jail for a trial, Zenger finally would be freed.

No one expected Cosby's next move.

Attorney General Richard Bradley, a Cosby supporter, charged Peter Zenger with an information. An *information* is like an indictment. One difference is that the attorney general, not a grand jury, makes the charge. Peter Zenger would remain in jail.

The information stated that Zenger had printed and published "false, malicious, seditious [and] scandalous" libel in two issues of the *Journal*.

The first issue appeared a year before on January 28, 1733/34. It said: "THE PEOPLE of this City and Province . . . *think, as Matters now stand, that their*

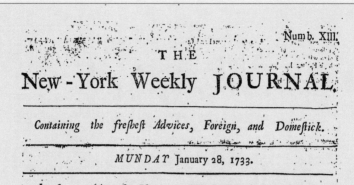

Numb. XIII.

THE
New-York Weekly JOURNAL

Containing the freshest Advices, Foreign, and Domestick.

MUNDAY January 28, 1733.

Lege frænata omnis potestas Esto;
BRACTON.

SIR,

MEN in a Torrent of Prosperity seldom think of a Day of Distress, or Great Men that their greatness will ever Cease. This seems to be a Sort of a Curse upon Power, a Vanity and Infatuation blended with the Nature of it: As if it were Possible nay easy to bind the Fickleness of Fortune, and ensure Happyness for a Term of Years. Tis from this Assureance, often cleaving to very able Men that those in Authority often act with such Boldness and, Insolence, as, if their Reign were never to End, and they were for ever secure against all After-reckonings, all casualties and disgrace. From whence else comes it, but from such blindSecurity in the Permanence of their Condition, and in the Impunity of their Actions, that Ministers have sometimes concerted SCHEMES OF GENERAL OPPRESSION AND PILLAGE, SCHEMES TO DEPRECIATE OR EVADE THE LAWs, RESTRAINTS UPON LIBERTY AND PROIECTS FOR ARBITRARY WILL? Had they thought that ever they themselves should suffer in the common Oppression would they have advised *Methods of Oppressing?* Should they have been for *Weakning* or *abrogating the Laws*, had they Dreamed that they should come to want THE PROTECTION OF THE LAW? Would they have aimed at *Abolishing Liberty*, had they apprehended that they were at any time to fall from Power; or at establishing *despotick Rule*, but for the Sake of *having the Direction of it* against others, without feeling ITS Weight and Terrors in their own Particulars?

How few Men in Power have secured to themselves a Resource of Friendship and Affection from the Publick, in Case of a Storm at Court and the Frowns of a Croun! Nay what some of them have done to serve the Crown against the People, has been a Motive with the Crown (and a politic Motive, tho not always a just one, at least not generous) to Sacrifice them to the Pleasure and Revenge of the People, thus *Cæsar Borgia*, used *Romiro D'orco* Governour of *Ramagna*, one first employed to commit Cruelties then executed for having committed them. Thus were EMPSON and DUDLEY used, and thus the great Turk often uses his Bashaws.

The GENERAL SECURITY, is the only certain Security of particulars; and tho'DesperateMen often find safety in publick Destruction, yet they cannot insure the same safety to their Children, who must suffer with the rest in the misery of all. If Great wicked Men would consider this, the World would not be plagued with their Ambition, their Posterity scarce ever miss to reap the bitter Fruits of their Actions, and the Curse of their iniquities rarely fails to follow them to the third and fourth Generation:

The INSTRUMENTS OF PUBLICK RUIN have generally at once intailed misery upon their Country and their own Race. Those who were the Instruments and Ministers of *Cæsar* and *Augustus*, and put the Common Wealth under their Feet AND THEM ABOVE THE LAWS, did not consider that they were not only forging Chains for their Country, but whetting Swords against their own Families; who were all cut off under succeeding Tyrants: Nay, most of their Children fell early

Seditious Words? Zenger was brought to trial for publishing "false, malicious, seditious [and] scandalous" libel in two issues of the New-York Weekly Journal—January 28, 1733/34, and April 8, 1734.

LIBERTIES *and* PROPERTIES *are precarious, and that* SLAVERY *is like to be entailed on them and their Posterity, if some past Things be not amended."*

The second issue was published on April 8, 1734. It reminded readers of Cosby's misdeeds: demanding salary payment from Rip Van Dam, setting up a special court without a jury to sue Van Dam, and removing Lewis Morris as supreme court justice.

Governor Cosby and his allies claimed that these attacks on the government were designed to cause public unrest. That made them seditious libels.

Many New Yorkers did not like the government using an information instead of a grand jury to charge Zenger. They thought it was unfair. After all, three grand juries had refused to indict the printer. If Governor Cosby and his friends could use their power to do this to Peter Zenger, what would stop them from doing it to other New Yorkers?

April 1735: Disbarred!

Zenger was not scheduled to appear in court again for more than two months. In April his lawyers, James Alexander and William Smith, presented their arguments in his defense.

According to Alexander and Smith, Judges James De Lancey and Frederick Philipse had no right to hear the printer's case. One reason, the lawyers argued, was that the Provincial Council had not approved Lewis Morris's removal from the Supreme Court. Nor did the Council approve the promotions of De Lancey and Philipse to chief and second judge. It had been illegal for Governor Cosby to make these changes without the Council's consent.

Judge De Lancey glared at the two lawyers from his bench in the front of the courtroom. "Consider the consequences of what [you] offered," he said sharply.

Both lawyers replied that they had well considered the consequences of what they said. Speaking passionately, William Smith announced that he was so sure of his argument that he would stake his life on it.

Judge De Lancey had no intention of stepping down as chief justice. It was Alexander and Smith who would lose their positions.

The Complaint of *James Alexander* and *William Smith* to the Committee of the General Aſſembly of the Colony of *New-York, &c.*

Mr. Chairman ;

§ I. IT is with the utmoſt Regret, that we attend this Committee in the Quality of Complainants ; but the Matter of it too nearly affects us and the Liberties of this Country, to be buried in Silence. Had our perſonal Intereſts been ſolely concerned, we might have reſted in a patient Expectation of a perſonal Remedy in ſome other Way : But when the Liberties of a Country are at Stake, and the Civil Enjoyments of a People ſap'd at the very Foundation of them, it behoves every Man that loves his Country to cry out and give publick *Warning of the Danger.* This Duty incumbent upon all, engages us in particular, to inform you, That in the Term of *April* laſt, we, in the Caſe of *John Peter Zenger,* then depending in the Supreme Court, filed Exceptions to the Commiſſions of the Juſtices theſe : The Tenour whereof follows.

The Attorney General, }
against } Upon an Information for a Miſdemeanour.
John Peter Zenger. }

Exceptions humbly offered by *John Peter Zenger,* to the Power of the Honourable *James De Lancey,* Eſq; to judge in this Cauſe.

The Defendant comes and prays Hearing of the Commiſſion, by Virtue of which the Honourable *James De Lancey,* Eſq; claims the Power and Authority to judge in this Cauſe, and it is read unto him in theſe Words;

'GEORGE the ſecond, by the Grace of God, of 'Great Britain, France & Ireland, King, Defender 'of the Faith, &c. To our truſty & welbeloved *James* 'De Lancey, Eſq; Greeting We repoſing eſpecial Truſt & 'Confidence in your Integrity, Ability & Learning, have 'aſſigned, conſtituted and appointed, and We do by 'theſe Preſents aſſign, conſtitute and appoint you the ſaid '*James De Lancey,* to be Chief Juſtice in and over 'our Province of *New-York,* in America, in the Room 'of *Lewis Morris,* Eſq; Giving and by theſe Preſents 'granting unto you, full Power and lawful Authority, 'to hear, try and determine all Pleas whatſoever, civil, 'criminal and mixt, according to the Laws, Statutes 'and Customs of Our Kingdom of England, and the 'Laws and Uſages of Our ſaid Province of New-York, 'not being repugnant thereto, and Execution of all 'Judgments of the ſaid Court to award, and to make

'ſuch Rules and Orders in the ſaid Court, as may be 'found convenient and uſeful, and as near as may be a-'greeable to the Rules and Orders of Our Courts of 'King's Bench, Common Pleas, and Exchequer in Eng-'land. To have held and enjoy the ſaid Office or Place 'of Chief Juſtice in and over Our ſaid Province, with 'all and ſingular the Rights, Priviledges Profits 'Advantages, Salaries, Fees and Perquiſites unto the 'ſaid Place belonging, or in any Ways appertaining, in 'as full and ample Manner as any Perſon heretofore 'Chief Juſtice of Our ſaid Province hath held and en-'joyed, or of Right, ought to have held and enjoyed the 'ſame, To you the ſaid James De Lancey, for and 'DURING OUR WILL AND PLEASURE. In 'Teſtimony whereof We have cauſed theſe Our Letters to 'be made Patent, and the great Seal of Our ſaid Pro-'vince of New-York to be hereunto affix'd. Witneſs 'Our truſty and welbeloved William Cosby, Eſq; Our 'Captain General and Governour in Chief of Our Pro-'vinces of New-York, New-Jerſey, and Terri-'tories thereon depending in America, Vice Admiral of 'the ſame, & Colonel in Our Army, &c. at Fort George 'in New-York, the Twenty firſt Day of Auguſt, in the 'ſeventh Year of Our Reign, & Anno Domini, 1733.

Which being read and heard, the ſaid *John Peter Zenger,* by Proteſtation not confeſſing nor ſubmitt-ing

A

Alexander and Smith Protest Their Disbarment In December 1735, James Alexander and William Smith made a formal complaint to the New York General Assembly about their disbarment from the Supreme Court the previous April. They asked the Assembly to overturn the action by Judges De Lancey and Philipse, arguing that it was unjust.

"You have brought it to that point that either we [De Lancey and Philipse] must go from the bench, or you from the bar," De Lancey said. As of that moment, the two lawyers would no longer have the right to practice law in the New York Supreme Court.

Alexander and Smith were stunned. They knew that they had made a bold move by challenging the judges' positions on the court. But they didn't expect De Lancey to disbar them.

With his lawyers unable to represent him, could things be worse for Peter Zenger? Few attorneys practiced law in New York in those days. Among them, Alexander and Smith were two of the most skilled. Many of the others had political ties to Governor Cosby.

Zenger immediately asked the judge to appoint a new attorney to defend him, as was his right. Judge De Lancey chose John Chambers. Chambers had been appointed by Cosby to be Recorder of the City, a political job. He also had run for New York Common Council in September 1734 as a Cosby supporter but lost. Zenger didn't expect much help from him.

Zenger's trial would not be held until August 4, nearly four months away. Until then, he would have to remain in prison. If the trial went badly, he could end up spending many years there.

The printer was tired of the endless legal struggle, tired of worrying about his family and his printing press, tired of the view from his cell. Even though the snowy New York winter was finally over, spring rains brought Zenger new misery. The roof over his attic jail cell leaked.

On May 1 Zenger and John Peeck, a fellow prisoner, sent a request to the city government asking for the roof to be fixed: "With every Rain your Petitioners [Zenger and Peeck] are not only much discomoded, their Healths endangered, but other inconveniences may be expected. The Windows also are so much shattered that your Petitioners are not able to keep out the Winds."

Governor Cosby might have hoped that Zenger would try to cut a deal to make things better for himself. It is possible that the governor offered the printer his freedom in return for the names of the men behind the *Journal*'s words. Those

A Leaky Jail Roof Peter Zenger and another prisoner sent this petition to the city government on May 1, 1735, asking for the repair of the leaky roof above their attic cell. The original document is among the historical records in the New York City Municipal Archives.

were the people Cosby wanted in jail. They—not Zenger—were his real enemies. Historians have no record of any such offer, however. What is known is that Zenger never squealed.

July 1735: Picking a Jury

Six days before Peter Zenger's trial began, a jury for the case had to be chosen. The court clerk was supposed to present a list of forty-eight names of possible jurors. These names were to be selected from all adult male property owners and voters in New York City. The lawyers from both sides would agree on twelve men from the list to make up the jury.

On Tuesday evening at five o'clock, the clerk produced the list. Peter Zenger's friends in the courtroom recognized the names. They were men with close ties to the governor, including Cosby's baker, tailor, and shoemaker. Some of the listed men weren't even allowed to sit on a jury because they were not property owners or voters.

Everyone realized what was going on. Governor Cosby's allies were trying to fill the jury with men who would find Peter Zenger guilty. The court clerk who chose the names owed his job to Cosby. By trying to fix the jury, he had done the governor's dirty work.

John Chambers, Peter Zenger's assigned lawyer, protested. Although Chambers was a Cosby ally, he could not let the legal system be corrupted in this way. He insisted that a new list of eligible jurors be drawn up.

Judge De Lancey agreed. The judge wanted Zenger to be found guilty, but Chambers was right. Zenger was entitled to a fairly chosen jury.

Peter Zenger felt better when the jury was finally selected. It turned out that at least half of the twelve jurors had ties to the Morrisites. But that didn't mean Zenger could count on being found innocent.

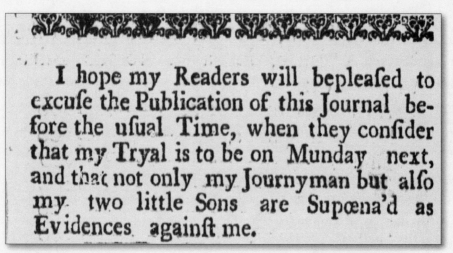

I hope my Readers will bepleafed to excufe the Publication of this Journal before the ufual Time, when they confider that my Tryal is to be on Munday next, and that not only my Journyman but alfo my two little Sons are Supœna'd as Evidences againft me.

A Special Trial-Week Edition *Notice from the* New-York Weekly Journal, *August 2, 1735. Zenger's trial was scheduled for a Monday, the day that the* New-York Weekly Journal *usually appeared. That week, the newspaper came out on Saturday instead. The notice explained that Zenger's journeyman and two sons, evidently key to publishing the newspaper on time, were to testify at the trial. The early publication also helped to remind readers of the trial date. On Monday, the courtroom was crowded with spectators.*

SEVEN

The Trial
"It is the cause of liberty"

James Alexander and William Smith had not abandoned Peter Zenger. After Judge De Lancey disbarred the two attorneys in April, the men searched for another lawyer to defend the printer. They couldn't trust John Chambers to do a good job. Not only was he young and inexperienced, but he was also a member of the Court Party.

Alexander had a friend in Philadelphia. He was a lawyer who sometimes borrowed law books from Alexander's library. Andrew Hamilton was one of the most famous and respected attorneys in the colonies. He agreed to take the printer's case.

The Morrisites made arrangements for Hamilton to come to New York for the trial. Few people knew about their plan. They wanted Hamilton's appearance in the courtroom to be a surprise, particularly to Governor Cosby and his supporters.

MONDAY, AUGUST 4, 1735: TRIAL DAY

Summer light streamed through the tall windows of the courtroom on the second floor of City Hall. The crowded room was hot and stuffy.

Wooden benches for the public spectators were filled. Those who could not find a seat stood shoulder to shoulder across the back and sides of the courtroom. Thanks to the *Journal*'s articles, New Yorkers had a strong interest in the Zenger case. As the trial continued, it became clear that most people present were sympathetic toward Peter Zenger.

Judges De Lancey and Philipse, wearing curly white wigs, peered down from the judicial bench between the windows. Attorney General Richard Bradley and Zenger's lawyer, John Chambers, collected their notes and law books on the tables

ANDREW HAMILTON
(1676–1741)

When the Morrisites asked Andrew Hamilton to defend Peter Zenger, they knew what they were doing. Hamilton was a brilliant lawyer. William Smith's son later described Hamilton in his *The History of the Province of New-York*: "He had art, eloquence, vivacity, and humour, was ambitious of fame, negligent of nothing to ensure success, and possessed a confidence which no terrors could awe."

Hamilton had come to America from Scotland when he was about twenty-one years old. Besides being a lawyer, Hamilton was an important political figure in Pennsylvania and held several government posts. Andrew Hamilton died on the sixth anniversary of the Zenger trial—August 4, 1741.

facing the judges. The jury of twelve men sat on benches to one side. Peter Zenger watched from the dock, a separate box in the courtroom where the accused stood.

James Alexander and William Smith were both in the courtroom, too. Because of their disbarment, however, they could not participate in the trial.

The trial began with Attorney General Bradley addressing the judges and jury. "Defendant Zenger has pleaded *not guilty*," said Bradley. He described the charge of "printing and publishing a *false, scandalous and seditious libel*" against Governor Cosby.

Next John Chambers gave an opening speech on Peter Zenger's behalf. Historians have found the notes that Chambers made in preparation for the trial. It appears that he expected to defend Zenger for the entire trial and did not know about Andrew Hamilton.

In his opening statement, Chambers declared that the attorney general must prove which specific person was, without doubt, the object of the *Journal*'s articles. Chambers planned to show that this could not be proved. Therefore, the charge of seditious libel would not hold.

Andrew Hamilton Appears

As Chambers returned to the lawyers' table, Andrew Hamilton dramatically stepped forward from among the spectators. In a forceful voice, he informed Judge De Lancey that he would be part of Zenger's defense.

A murmur swept through the courtroom. The Philadelphian was well known in legal circles. The attorney general and the two judges suddenly realized that the trial would not go as smoothly as they had expected.

Hamilton was fifty-nine. He was not a healthy man, however, and he looked older. Though slow moving, Hamilton had a strong voice. The jurors, like everyone else in the courtroom, could not take their eyes off him when he spoke.

"I'll save Mr. Attorney [the attorney general] the trouble of examining his witnesses . . . ," Hamilton said. "I do (for my client) confess that he both printed and published the two newspapers set forth in the information, and I hope in so doing he has committed no crime."

The Trial *Andrew Hamilton argues Peter Zenger's case before Judges James De Lancey and Frederick Philipse on August 4, 1735. Peter Zenger stands in the dock next to a guard. This is an artist's guess of what the scene looked like. No known drawings exist of Zenger or of the courtroom that day. Historians aren't even certain that the judges and attorneys would have been wearing robes.*

Attorney General Bradley was caught off-guard. He had been ready to show that Zenger was guilty of printing the newspapers. To prove this, Bradley had gathered witnesses, including Peter Zenger's journeyman and two sons. He wouldn't need them now.

Bradley didn't know what to say next. The jury's job was to decide if Zenger had printed the *Journal*. Zenger had just admitted doing that. Bradley figured the trial was over.

The courtroom was silent.

Finally, Judge De Lancey addressed Bradley. "Well Mr. Attorney, will you proceed?"

Bradley turned to the two judges. "I think the jury must find a verdict for the King."

"Not so . . . , Mr. Attorney," Hamilton interjected. "You will have something more to do before you make my client a libeler; for the words themselves must be libelous, that is, *false, scandalous, and seditious* or else we are not guilty."

Hamilton was arguing that since the charge against Zenger stated the newspaper articles were false, it was up to the prosecution to *prove* that they were false.

The Defense Strategy

Before the trial, James Alexander and William Smith had mapped out the legal strategy for Zenger's defense. They had given Hamilton notes for his presentation. Many of the arguments in their notes had been printed in the *Journal*'s essays during the previous months.

The lawyers knew that the law was against Zenger. He had printed the *Journal*; his name was on every issue of the newspaper. According to the law, only the judges were allowed to decide if the newspaper articles were libelous. Since Judges De Lancey and Philipse were both Cosby allies, there was no doubt what they would decide. Zenger would be convicted.

The only hope was to persuade the jury to vote that Zenger was not guilty of printing the newspaper articles. By doing that, the jury would prevent the judges from being able to rule on whether the material was libelous. Zenger would go free.

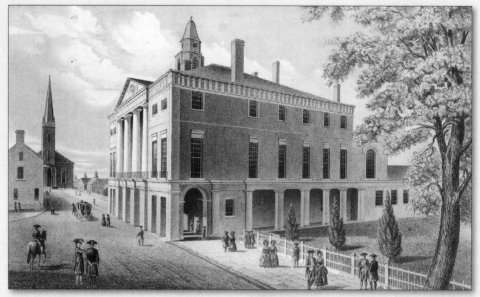

Federal Hall, 1789 *After the United States Constitution was ratified in 1788, New York City served as the nation's capital until 1790, when the federal government moved to Philadelphia. New York City Hall, site of John Peter Zenger's trial, was remodeled to house the new government and was renamed Federal Hall. On April 30, 1789, George Washington took the first presidential oath on the second-floor balcony behind the white columns. The first Congress met in the building, where it adopted the Bill of Rights. Trinity Church is visible two blocks away.*

Federal Hall National Memorial, 2005 *This building, now a national park, was constructed on the site of the original City Hall/Federal Hall and opened in 1842. A statue of George Washington stands at the entrance. When this photograph was taken, the building was closed to visitors for repairs. The foundation had been damaged on September 11, 2001, by intense ground vibrations caused by the collapse of the World Trade Center towers a few blocks away. The flag is at half-mast in memory of the victims of Hurricane Katrina, the August 2005 storm that flooded New Orleans and the Gulf Coast.*

This was the strategy that Andrew Hamilton followed as the trial continued. He and Attorney General Bradley argued back and forth. Bradley said that under English law, an attack on a person was libel whether it was true or false.

Hamilton disagreed. He said that the libel laws of England should not be the law in New York. "What is good law at one time and in one place is not so at another time and in another place." Hamilton argued that a free press was the only thing that could protect colonists from corrupt governors. These officials were too far away from England to be controlled by the king.

Then Hamilton emphasized the heart of the defense: The articles printed in the two issues of the *Journal* were true. True articles are not libelous. Therefore, Zenger is not guilty of seditious libel. "We are ready to prove them to be true," Hamilton announced.

Attorney General Bradley objected: If a libel has been published—which Zenger has just admitted—then it doesn't matter whether it is true or false.

The last thing Judge De Lancey wanted was a parade of people testifying about Governor Cosby's misdeeds. He did not allow Hamilton to call witnesses to prove that the printed statements were true.

Hamilton Makes His Case

Hamilton saw that the judge would not let him stick with the original strategy. The quick-thinking lawyer changed his approach. Turning toward the jury, he spoke directly to the twelve men: You know that the *Journal's* articles attacking Governor Cosby and his administration "are notoriously known to be true."

Judge De Lancey tried to stop Hamilton. "No, Mr. Hamilton," he said. "The jury may find that Zenger printed and published those papers, and leave to the Court to judge whether they are libelous."

Despite having the law on his side, the young judge was no match for Andrew Hamilton's skill, confidence, and knowledge. The lawyer from Philadelphia would not give in. Ignoring Judge De Lancey, Hamilton continued to speak to the jury.

He told the men that they had the right to decide both parts—whether Zenger had printed the articles *and* whether the articles were libelous. "If you should be

Building the Cradle of Liberty *Andrew Hamilton, in white wig, inspects the partially built Pennsylvania State House in Philadelphia, now known as Independence Hall. Hamilton oversaw construction of the building, beginning in 1732, while he was a member of the Pennsylvania Assembly. It was in this landmark that both the Declaration of Independence and the United States Constitution were approved.* Building the Cradle of Liberty *was painted in the early 1900s by American artist Jean Leon Gerome Ferris (1863–1930).*

of opinion that there is no falsehood in Mr. Zenger's papers . . . you ought to say so . . . It is your right to do so, and there is much depending upon your resolution as well as upon your integrity."

Hamilton's speech was spellbinding. When he made strong points, the spectators in the courtroom cheered.

He continued, "The question before the Court and you gentlemen of the jury . . . is not the cause of a poor printer, nor of New York alone, which you are now trying: No! It may in its consequence affect every freeman that lives under a British government on the main of America. It is the best cause. It is the cause of liberty."

In ending his address to the jury, Hamilton reminded the men of the importance of their decision. By finding John Peter Zenger innocent, they would help fellow citizens now and in the future have the freedom of "exposing and opposing arbitrary power . . . by speaking and writing truth."

When Hamilton was through, Judge De Lancey told the jury to ignore what the lawyer had said. The judge repeated the law: the jury's only job was to decide if Zenger had printed and published the newspaper.

The jury had its own ideas. Hamilton had struck a nerve with the twelve men. Only ten minutes after they had left the courtroom to make their decision, the jury returned.

The court clerk asked for the jury's verdict.

Thomas Hunt, the jury foreman, replied, "Not Guilty."

"Huzza! Huzza! Huzza!" cheered the crowd in the courtroom.

Cadwallader Colden reported: "scarcely one person except the officers of the Court were observ'd not to join in this noisy exclamation."

Judge De Lancey demanded order in the courtroom and threatened to jail those who didn't quiet down. After no one listened to him, De Lancey hurried from the courtroom with Judge Philipse at his heels.

XCIII.

THE
New-York Weekly JOURNAL.

Containing the freſheſt Advices, Foreign, and Domeſtick.

MUNDAY Auguſt 18th, 1735.

To my Subſcribers and Benefactors.

Gentlemen ;

I Think my ſelf in Duty bound to to make publick Acknowledgment for the many Favours received at your Hands, which I do in this Manner return you my hearty Thanks for. I very ſoon intend to print my Tryal at Length, that the World may ſee how unjuſt my Sufferings have been, ſo will only at this Time give this ſhort Account of it.

On *Munday* the 4th Inſtant my Tryal for Printing Parts of my Journal No. 13. and 23. came on, in the Supreme Court of this Province, before the moſt numerous Auditory of People, I may with Juſtice ſay, that ever were ſeen in that Place at once ; my Jury ſworn were;

1 *Harmanus Rutgers,*
2 *Stanley Holms,*
3 *Edward Man,*
4 *John Bell,*
5 *Samuel Weaver,*
6 *Andrew Marſchalk,*
7 *Egbert Van Borſen,*
8 *Thomas Hunt,*
9 *Benjamin Hildrith,*
10 *Abraham Kitcltaſs,*
11 *John Goelet,*
12 *Hercules Wendover,*

John Chambers, Eſq; had been appointed the Term before by the Court as my Council, in the Place of *James Alexander* and *William Smith,* who were then ſilenced on my Account, and to Mr. *Chambers*'s Aſſiſtance came *Andrew Hamilton,* Eſq; of *Philadelphia* Barreſter at Law ; when Mr Attorney offered the Information and the Proofs, Mr. *Hamilton* told him, he would acknowledge my Printing and Publiſhing the Papers in the Information, and ſave him the Trouble of that Proof, and offered to prove the Facts of thoſe Papers true, and had Witneſſes ready to prove every Fact ; he long inſiſted on the Liberty of Making Proof thereof, but was over-ruled therein. Mr. Attorney offered no Proofs of my Papers being *falſe, malicious* and *ſeditious,* as they were charged to be, but inſiſted that they were Lybels tho' true. There were many Arguments and Authorities on this point, and the Court were of Opinion with Mr. Attorney on that Head : But the Jury having taken the Information out with them, they returned in about Ten Minutes, and found me *Not Guilty* ; upon which there were immediately three Hurra's of many Hundreds of People in the preſence of the Court, before the Verdict was returned. The next Morning my Diſcharge was moved for and granted, and ſufficient was ſub-

Thanks to Supporters The New-York Weekly Journal's *August 18, 1735,* issue contained a summary of the trial and a notice from Zenger: "To my Subscribers and Benefactors. Gentlemen; I Think my self in Duty bound to so make publick Acknowledgment for the many Favours received at your Hands, which I do in this Manner return you my hearty Thanks for. I very soon intend to print my Tryal at Length, that the World may see how unjust my Sufferings have been, so will only at this Time give this short Account of it."

Celebration

The celebration in the courtroom spilled into the street. Yet Peter Zenger could not join the party. Despite being found innocent, he spent the night in jail. Judge De Lancey had left the courtroom before formally freeing the printer.

In addition, the court required that before being released, Zenger must pay for his food and shelter during his stay in jail. In New York at this time, such was the rule for prisoners. The next morning, Zenger's supporters paid the fees. By noon, the printer was a free man again.

Andrew Hamilton became a hero for his magnificent defense of Peter Zenger. The next day, when Hamilton headed back to Philadelphia, ships in New York Harbor saluted him with their cannons. A few weeks later, the New York City Common Council honored Hamilton with a declaration in appreciation for "his Learned and generous Defence of the Rights of Mankind, and the Liberty of the Press."

In its August 18 issue, the *Journal* listed the jurors' names and thanked them for their decision. Their verdict ended Governor Cosby's efforts to silence the *Journal*. The Morrisites had won an important battle against Cosby and his supporters.

The cost of the fight had been high for one man, though. Peter Zenger had sacrificed nearly nine months of his life in the City Hall jail for printing the Morrisites' words. Yet despite his sacrifice, the Morrisites had not delayed their celebration until Zenger was released from jail and could join them. The celebration, it seemed, had more to do with political victory than with a printer's freedom.

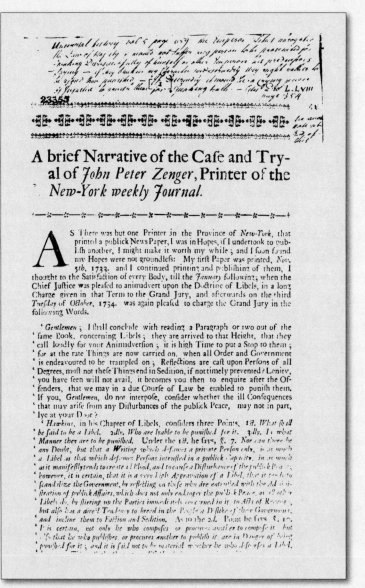

A brief Narrative of the Case and Tryal of *John Peter Zenger*, Printer of the *New-York weekly Journal.*

AS There was but one Printer in the Province of *New-York*, that printed a publick News Paper, I was in Hopes, if I undertook to publish another, I might make it worth my while ; and I soon found my Hopes were not groundless: My first Paper was printed, *Nov. 5th, 1733.* and I continued printing and publishing of them, I thought to the Satisfaction of every Body, till the *January* following; when the Chief Justice was pleased to animadvert upon the Doctrine of Libels, in a long Charge given in that Term to the Grand Jury, and afterwards on the third *Tuesday of October, 1734.* was again pleased to charge the Grand Jury in the following Words.

' *Gentlemen* ; I shall conclude with reading a Paragraph or two out of the
' same Book, concerning Libels ; they are arrived to that Height, that they
' call loudly for your Animadversion ; it is high Time to put a Stop to them ;
' for at the rate Things are now carried on, when all Order and Government
' is endeavoured to be trampled on ; Reflections are cast upon Persons of all
' Degrees, must not these Things end in Sedition, if not timely prevented? Lenity,
' you have seen will not avail, it becomes you then to enquire after the Of-
' fenders, that we may in a due Course of Law be enabled to punish them.
' If you, *Gentlemen*, do not interpose, consider whether the ill Consequences
' that may arise from any Disturbances of the publick Peace, may not in part,
' lye at your Door?

' *Hawkins*, in his Chapter of Libels, considers three Points, 1*st*. *What shall*
' *be said to be a Libel.* 2*dly*. *Who are liable to be punished for it.* 3*dly*. *In what*
' *Manner they are to be punished.* Under the 1*st*, he says, §. 7. *Nor can there be*
' *any Doubt, but that a Writing which defames a private Person only, is as much*
' *a Libel as that which defames Persons intrusted in a publick Capacity, in as much*
' *as it manifestly tends to create ill Blood, and to cause a Disturbance of the publick Peace ;*
' *however, it is certain, that it is a very high Aggravation of a Libel, that it tends to to*
' *scandalize the Government, by reflecting on those who are entrusted with the Adminis-*
' *stration of publick Affairs, which does not only endanger the publick Peace, as all other*
' *Libels do, by stirring up the Parties immediately concerned in it, to Acts of Revenge,*
' *but also has a direct Tendency to breed in the People a Dislike of their Governours,*
' *and incline them to Faction and Sedition.* As to the 2*d*. Point he says §. 10.
' *It is certain, not only he who composes or procures another to compose it, but*
' *also that he who publishes, or procures another to publish it, are in Danger of being*
' *punished for it ; and it is said not to be material whether he who disperses a Libel,*

A Brief Narrative, 1736 *Page 1 from the first edition of* A Brief Narrative of the Case and Tryal of John Peter Zenger, Printer of the New-York Weekly Journal. *The forty-page pamphlet was written by James Alexander and printed and sold in late spring 1736 by Peter Zenger. The handwritten notes at the top of the page were made later, perhaps by a historian or librarian.*

EIGHT

What Happened Afterward

"THE FREEDOM OF SPEECH is a principal pillar in a free government"

A BRIEF NARRATIVE

In late spring 1736, Peter Zenger printed and sold a forty-page pamphlet about the trial, called *A Brief Narrative of the Case and Tryal of John Peter Zenger, Printer of the New-York Weekly Journal*. Although *A Brief Narrative* was written as if Zenger were the author, the words came from James Alexander's pen. Andrew Hamilton's trial notes were also included. Zenger's contribution was only as printer and publisher.

A Brief Narrative was reprinted in Boston and London two years later. By 1800, it had been reprinted fifteen times and distributed throughout the colonies and Great Britain.

The pamphlet's wide circulation influenced the attitudes of future generations of colonial Americans. Discontent in the colonies increased in the 1760s after Britain increased taxes and restricted trade. Those who pushed for revolution believed the Zenger trial proved that they were right to oppose British rule. After independence from Great Britain was won, the first United States Congress included guarantees of a free press in the Bill of Rights.

JAMES ALEXANDER

The driving force behind the Zenger case was James Alexander. He continued his passionate arguments for a free press years after the trial ended. Through his writings and his legal and political tactics, he turned the case of the imprisoned printer into a call for freedom. That call has been remembered over the span of nearly three centuries.

After the trial, Alexander and William Smith asked the Assembly to let them

Trinity Church, 1737. *Many colonial leaders, including James Alexander and William Bradford, attended religious services at Trinity Church at Broadway and Wall Street. The original church was destroyed in a 1776 fire that also burned down five hundred houses.*

Trinity Church, 2005. *After the second Trinity Church building was torn down in 1839, the present Neo-Gothic-style structure was built on the same site.*

James Alexander's Weathered Gravestone *on the west side of Trinity Church cemetery.*

practice law again in the New York Supreme Court. In 1737, their request was granted. Both had long political careers.

Alexander died at age sixty-four and was buried in the Trinity Church cemetery, New York City. He left behind mountains of notes and papers from his career. Historians have learned much about colonial New York and New Jersey from Alexander's writings. His papers provide details about the birth of the *New-York Weekly Journal* and about the Zenger case.

GOVERNOR WILLIAM COSBY

Governor Cosby lived only seven months after the Zenger trial. He died on March 10, 1735/36.

Historical accounts say that Cosby had a lung disease, perhaps tuberculosis. The governor had apparently been ill for several months. In December 1735, James Alexander wrote to Lewis Morris, who was still in England, and reported that Cosby suffered from a persistent fever. In a March 1735/36 letter, Provincial Council member George Clarke informed the Duke of Newcastle that Cosby had died after a sixteen-week sickness. Clarke took over as acting governor following Cosby's death.

Cosby's lawsuit against Rip Van Dam was never settled. Yet it was this lawsuit that kicked off the chain of events leading to the *Journal*'s birth and to John Peter Zenger's important trial.

Rip Van Dam died June 10, 1749, long outliving his bitter foe.

JOHN PETER ZENGER

After Peter Zenger was released from jail, he went back to printing the four-page *Journal*. Essays about liberty continued next to news from Europe and the other colonies. Articles appeared about Lewis Morris's trip to London and about the Morrisites' disagreements with the government.

The Morrisites gained political power in the elections after Cosby's death. Thanks to this, Zenger became the official government printer in New York and New Jersey in 1737 and 1738. The positions were eventually given back to William

> ALL those that are Indebted to the NEW-YORK Weekly JOURNAL above one Year, are desired to send in their Arrearage, thereby to enable the Printer to continue Publishing this Paper.

Please Pay Your Bills On the day of Peter Zenger's death, July 28, 1746, a notice appeared in the New-York Weekly Journal asking for overdue payments from customers.

> MY Country Subscribers are earnestly desired to Pay their Arrearages for this Journal, which, if they don't do speedily, shall leave off sending; and seek my Money another way: Some of these kind Subscribers are in Arrear upwords of seven Years! Now, as I have serv'd them so long, I think it is Time, Ay, and high time too, that they give me my Outsett, for they may verily believe that my every Day Cloaths are almost worne out.

The Final Journal Financial problems continued to plague the Zengers. In the last known issue of the Journal—18 March 1750/51—publisher John Zenger (Peter Zenger's son) pleaded with subscribers to pay their bills.

A Grave Error William Bradford's grave is on the north side of Trinity Church cemetery in New York City. Although Bradford spent his life trying to avoid printing errors, his gravestone was engraved with mistakes. He was born in 1663, but the grave marker reads 1660. Bradford was actually eighty-nine when he died, not ninety-two as the inscription reads. In 1863, a new stone was erected to replace the weathered original. But cemetery rules required the replacement to match the original—mistakes and all.

The beginning of the inscription reads: "Here lies the Body of Mr. WILLIAM BRADFORD Printer, who departed this Life May 23, 1752, aged 92 Years. He was born in Leicestershire, in Old England, in 1660 and came over to America in 1682, before the City of Philadelphia was laid out. He was Printer to this Government for upwards of 50 Years."

Bradford, however. The political tides changed, and perhaps Zenger fell from favor. Or maybe his work was not satisfactory.

The son of William Smith, one of Zenger's lawyers, later wrote a history of New York. In it, he said that after the trial, Zenger handled his fame poorly. The excessive praise the printer received from the public made him lazy "and ended, as the ferment subsided, in the ruin of his family."

Peter Zenger died on July 28, 1746. He left his wife Catharine and six children. For two years after his death, his widow published the *Journal* and managed the printing shop. It is likely that Zenger's sons, not she, did the actual printing.

At the end of 1748, Catharine turned the newspaper over to Peter Zenger's son John from his first marriage. Things did not go well. In March 1750/51, John printed a plea in the *Journal* asking people who owed him money to pay their debts from as far back as seven years. Soon after, he went out of business. The *New-York Weekly Journal*, the newspaper that had shaken the foundations of British rule in New York, was no longer.

William Bradford

William Bradford had not enjoyed his role in the paper war between his *Gazette* and the *Journal*. After Governor Cosby died, Bradford told his *Gazette* readers that the Morrisites had been "very good Friends" before Cosby arrived. It hadn't been his plan to engage in "a Controversie or Paper War" with them. Bradford claimed he had been forced to publish the opinions of Cosby's supporters in his newspaper because he was the government printer.

William Bradford died in May 1752 at the age of eighty-nine. He is buried in the graveyard at Trinity Church, New York City, not far from James Alexander.

Judge Lewis Morris

Throughout the winter after Peter Zenger's trial, Lewis Morris remained in London. He eventually realized that he would not be able to convince the royal authorities to replace Cosby as governor. Only Cosby's death accomplished the Morrisites' goal.

It took several weeks for the news of the governor's death to cross the ocean to

Bill of Rights *The original document (shown here) is on display at the National Archives in Washington, D.C.*

THE BILL OF RIGHTS

The authors of the Constitution believed that government should be run by its citizens. The heart of democracy is the public's right to communicate opinion freely.

In 1789, the first United States Congress adopted a series of amendments to the Constitution proposed by James Madison of Virginia. By December 1791, ten of these amendments, now known as the Bill of Rights, had been approved by the states and became part of the Constitution. The amendments were designed to protect the rights of individual citizens.

The First Amendment included the guarantee of the right to express opinions through speech and the press:

"Congress shall make no law respecting an establishment of religion, or prohibiting the free exercise thereof; or abridging the freedom of speech, or of the press; or the right of the people peaceably to assemble, and to petition the Government for a redress of grievances."

Many people believe that the Zenger jury's verdict of "not guilty" was a victory for the idea of a free press. It is fitting, then, that the Bill of Rights was adopted by Congress in the same building where Peter Zenger had been jailed and tried more than fifty years before.

London. After that, Morris had no reason to stay. He returned to New York in the fall of 1736 to a large, welcoming crowd. Despite the applause, Morris's mission had not been successful. Although the Privy Council decided that Governor Cosby had been wrong to dismiss Morris from the New York Supreme Court, it did not recommend giving Morris back his judgeship.

Morris's political maneuvers in London seemed to pay off two years later, however. In 1738, the British granted New Jersey its own governor instead of sharing one with New York. Morris was given the position. He served as New Jersey's governor until his death in 1746. His son, Lewis Morris, Jr., remained active in New York politics.

Several of Lewis Morris's descendants played key roles in the founding of the new government of the United States. His grandson Gouverneur Morris (1752–1816) helped to write the United States Constitution. Gouverneur once said: "The trial of Zenger in 1735 was the germ of American freedom, the morning star of that liberty which subsequently revolutionized America."

Freedom of the Press

In his address to the Zenger jury, Andrew Hamilton argued for the right to publish truth about the government without facing punishment. If criticism was true, he said, it was not libelous. The jury agreed. Yet the Zenger trial did not change the law.

Legal changes came gradually over many decades. Today Americans have the right to criticize their government. Seditious libel is not considered an acceptable charge in American courts.

A printed statement about public officials is considered a libel only if it is an intended lie. Writers, editors, and publishers do not have to prove that their comments are true. Instead, public officials have to prove that the authors knew that the words were false.

What *did* change after the Zenger trial was the political atmosphere in the colonies. British governors were reluctant to charge American printers with seditious libel. They realized that colonial juries would refuse to convict anyone for publishing criticisms of royal officials.

Scene at the Signing of the Constitution of the United States *This 1940 painting by Howard Chandler Christy (1873–1952) shows the signing of the Constitution on September 17, 1787, in Philadelphia. It hangs in the U.S. Capitol. George Washington, who presided at the Constitutional Convention, stands at the desk. Two of the signers had close ties to men from the Zenger case more than fifty years earlier. Gouverneur Morris (Lewis Morris's grandson) stands in the center back, four to the left of the man with the raised arm and bent elbow. To the left of Morris, leaning over, is William Livingston. Livingston received his law training from James Alexander and William Smith. William Smith's son and James Alexander's daughter and son married into Livingston's family.*

Gouverneur Morris *(1752–1816), grandson of Lewis Morris, headed the committee that wrote the final draft of the United States Constitution. He later served as minister to France during George Washington's presidency and as a U.S. senator from New York.*

Because of this, the colonial press became more open and free. Printers in America published attacks on British rule as well as calls for independence. These words spread throughout the colonies and eventually led to the American Revolution.

The Zenger trial was a significant event in the fight for the citizens' right to criticize government. In 1737, James Alexander summed up the ideas that eventually found their way into the United States Constitution. In a letter to Benjamin Franklin's newspaper, the *Pennsylvania Gazette,* he wrote:

"THE FREEDOM OF SPEECH is a *principal pillar* in a free government: when this support is taken away the constitution is dissolved, and tyranny is erected on its ruins."

Timeline

1607
Jamestown, Virginia, becomes the first permanent English settlement in the present-day United States.

1620
English colonists, Pilgrims, settle in Plymouth, Massachusetts.

1624
Dutch colonists settle in New Netherland (now New York State).

1664
England takes control of New Netherland from the Dutch and changes the name to *New York*.

1689
A series of wars begins between England and France over control of North America. The wars continue off and on until 1763, with many of the battles occurring in the New York colony.

1710
German John Peter Zenger, age thirteen, immigrates to America with his family and becomes an apprentice to printer William Bradford in New York.

1715
James Alexander and William Smith meet on the ship from England as they both immigrate to New York.

1726
Zenger opens his own printing shop on Smith Street in New York.

1727
George II becomes king of England upon the death of his father, George I.

1732
August William Cosby arrives in New York as the province's new governor.

November Cosby demands that Rip Van Dam give him part of the salary that Van Dam earned as interim governor before Cosby's arrival. Van Dam refuses. Cosby decides to use the courts to get his money.

1733
March/April Lewis Morris, chief justice of the New York Supreme Court, states that the Supreme Court should not be used as a special court, without a jury, to hear Cosby's case against Van Dam.

August Governor Cosby removes Morris from the Supreme Court in retaliation for his ruling on the special court. He replaces Morris with James De Lancey, a Cosby supporter.

October Governor Cosby's allies rig an election for assemblyman so that Lewis Morris will lose. Morris wins anyway.

November The Morrisites hire Peter Zenger to publish and print their newspaper, the *New-York Weekly Journal*. James Alexander acts as editor. The first issue appears November 5.

1734
Throughout the year, the *Journal* prints articles that accuse Governor Cosby of abusing his power at the expense of New Yorkers.

January To silence the *Journal*, Governor Cosby gets Judge James De Lancey to ask a grand jury to indict Peter Zenger for publishing articles that criticize the government. The jury refuses because of lack of evidence.

October A second grand jury says it finds no evidence that Zenger published seditious articles.

Timeline

November 6 Copies of the *Journal* are burned in front of City Hall by the order of the Provincial Council.

November 17 Zenger is arrested for seditious libel and is imprisoned in the City Hall jail.

November 23 Lewis Morris leaves for London, where he plans to plead the Morrisites' case against Governor Cosby and his administration.

1735

January When a third grand jury refuses to indict Zenger for seditious libel because of the lack of evidence, the attorney general files an information. Zenger will face trial. The printer remains in prison.

April In court, James Alexander and William Smith question whether the two supreme court judges should be allowed to preside over the Zenger case. In response, Judge James De Lancey disbars both attorneys, forbidding them to represent Zenger in court. John Chambers, a Cosby ally, is assigned by the court to be Zenger's new lawyer. Not trusting Chambers, the Morrisites contact the famous Philadelphia lawyer Andrew Hamilton. Hamilton agrees to defend Zenger when the printer's case goes to trial.

July 29 Jury selection starts. John Chambers, still representing Zenger, prevents an attempt to fill the jury with Cosby supporters.

August 4 On the day of the trial, attorney Andrew Hamilton appears from Philadelphia to defend Zenger, surprising almost everyone. Thanks to Hamilton's spellbinding appeal for innocence, the jury declares Zenger "not guilty" of the charge of seditious libel. The next day Zenger is freed from prison after almost nine months.

1736

March Governor Cosby dies in New York.

Spring Zenger publishes the account of his trial, *A Brief Narrative of the Case and Tryal of John Peter Zenger*. It is written by James Alexander.

1765

British Parliament passes the Stamp Act, taxing American colonists for all printed material, including newspapers. Angry colonists protest.

1775–1783

The Revolutionary War is fought and the American colonies win their independence from Great Britain.

1776

The Declaration of Independence is adopted by the Second Continental Congress in Philadelphia.

1787

The United States Constitution is written and signed at the Constitutional Convention in Philadelphia.

1789

George Washington takes the oath of office as first president of the United States in Federal Hall (Old City Hall), New York City.

1791

The Bill of Rights is ratified by the states, becoming the first ten amendments to the U.S. Constitution.

Acknowledgments

This book would not have been possible without the help of experts who sent me in the right direction, filled in important blanks, and answered my questions.

For sharing their extensive knowledge of the Zenger case, my thanks to Professor Paul Finkelman of the University of Tulsa and Professor Stanley Katz of Princeton University. Professor Steven Shiffrin, a First Amendment expert at Cornell University Law School, explained the legal intricacies of libel. Professor Mary Beth Norton of Cornell University and Professor Serena Zabin of Carleton College provided information about colonial America.

I also welcomed the assistance of Remmel Nunn of Readex; Steve Laise of the National Park Service at Federal Hall National Memorial; Christine Jochem of the Morristown and Morris Township Library in New Jersey; and Kyle Jarrow, my Manhattan-savvy son.

I am grateful to my editor, Carolyn P. Yoder. I knew she would expect me to read more, probe deeper, and search further. So I did.

As I worked on this book, I became even more appreciative of our colonial rabble-rousers. Where would we be today if they had kept their voices silent and their feather pens still?

—G. J.

Further Reading

Books

For James Alexander's complete account of the Zenger case, see the following two books. The editors add legal background about the case and its impact on freedom of the press.

Finkelman, Paul, ed. *A Brief Narrative of the Case and Tryal of John Peter Zenger.* Union, NJ: The Lawbook Exchange, Ltd., 2000.

Katz, Stanley Nider, ed. *A Brief Narrative of the Case and Trial of John Peter Zenger.* 2nd ed. Cambridge, MA: Belknap Press of Harvard University Press, 1972.

For more about freedom of the press, the meaning of the Bill of Rights, and Supreme Court rulings related to the first ten amendments:

Freedman, Russell. *In Defense of Liberty: The Story of America's Bill of Rights.* New York: Holiday House, 2003.

Hudson, David L., Jr. *The Bill of Rights: The First Ten Amendments of the Constitution.* Berkeley Heights, NJ: Enslow Publishers, 2002.

King, David C. *The Right to Speak Out.* Brookfield, CT: Millbrook Press, 1997.

For information on the colonial history of New York:

Fradin, Dennis B. *The New York Colony.* Chicago: Children's Press, 1988.

Paulson, Timothy. *Life in the Thirteen Colonies.* New York: Children's Press, 2004.

For more on the history of the printing press and how it changed the world:

Heinrichs, Ann. *The Printing Press.* New York: Franklin Watts, 2005.

Meltzer, Milton. *The Printing Press.* New York: Benchmark Books, 2003.

For a novel about New York during the Zenger trial:

Krensky, Stephen. *The Printer's Apprentice.* New York: Delacorte Press, 1995.

Web Sites*

The Historical Society of the Courts of the State of New York. *The Trial of John Peter Zenger.* http://www.courts.state.ny.us/history/zenger.htm. Includes a readable copy of the 1736 *A Brief Narrative of the Case and Tryal of John Peter Zenger.*

Linder, Douglas, ed. *John Peter Zenger Trial 1735.* http://www.law.umkc.edu/faculty/projects/ftrials/zenger/ zenger.html. Linder is a professor of law at the University of Missouri–Kansas City School of Law. Web site contains images of key people and copies of documents. Of particular interest is the legal discussion of the First Amendment.

*Active at the time of publication

Places to Visit

Federal Hall, New York City
The National Park Service manages this historic building, built on the 1735 site of City Hall. http://www.nps.gov/feha.

Trinity Church, New York City
Trinity Church is located a few minutes from Federal Hall. Visit the graves of James Alexander and William Bradford. http://www.trinitywallstreet.org.

Colonial Williamsburg, Williamsburg, Virginia
Visit this restoration of an eighteenth-century city. At the printing office, watch experts demonstrate the same techniques used by John Peter Zenger. The Web site has information on the printing trade and colonial newspapers. http://www.history.org/Almanack/life/trades/tradepri.cfm.

Independence National Historical Park, Philadelphia, Pennsylvania
See Independence Hall, where the Founding Fathers debated and approved the Declaration of Independence and the U.S. Constitution. http://www.nps.gov/inde/home.htm.

A short distance away is Franklin Court, honoring Benjamin Franklin. For more about Franklin, including his work as a printer, see http://www.nps.gov/inde/Franklin_Court.

Visit the nearby National Constitution Center to learn about the writing of the Constitution, the Bill of Rights, and the Founding Fathers. http://www.constitutioncenter.org.

The National Archives, Washington, D.C.
Get an up-close view of the Declaration of Independence, the Constitution, and the Bill of Rights. http://www.archives.gov.

Notes

The quotations in this book come from historical documents. No dialogue is invented. The source of each quotation is found in the following notes. The citation indicates the first words of a quotation and its document source. The sources are listed in the bibliography.

Quotations match the source, including the misspellings and the capitalization style of the colonial author. In order to convey the drama of the trial scenes, however, Katz's version of *A Brief Narrative of the Case and Trial of John Peter Zenger* is used as the source for the courtroom dialogue. In this version, the spelling and capitalization of the 1736 pamphlet have been modernized to provide a more readable text.

Introduction   Page 8
"The basis of our governments . . .": letter from Jefferson to Edward Carrington, January 16, 1787.
    Papers of Thomas Jefferson, p. 49.

Chapter One   Page 14
"why they did not . . .": Colden, p. 288.
"I had more trouble . . .": letter from Cosby to Newcastle, October 26, 1732,
    Documents of New Jersey, p. 321.
"He was far from . . .": Colden, p. 299.
"mean, weak . . .": quoted in Sheridan, *Lewis Morris*, p. 152.
"depended neither upon . . .": quoted by James Alexander in a letter, March 19, 1732/33,
    Documents of New Jersey, p. 328.
"As to my Integrity . . .": *The Papers of Lewis Morris*, p. 50.
"It is evident . . .": Cosby in letter to Newcastle, May 3, 1733, *Documents of New York*, vol. 5, p. 948.
"I must either displace . . .": same as above, p. 949.

Chapter Two   Page 24
"How, gentleman, do you think . . .": quoted in Smith, p. 23.
"We Extreamly want . . .": letter from Alexander to Hunter, November 8, 1733,
    Documents of New Jersey, p. 360.
"Our Governour . . .": same as above, p. 359.
"There is one James . . .": letter from Cosby to Newcastle, December 18, 1732,
    Documents of New Jersey, p. 323.
"contrary to Law . . .": *New-York Weekly Journal*, November 5, 1733.
"Inclosed is also the first . . .": letter from Alexander to Hunter, November 8, 1733,
    Documents of New Jersey, p. 360.

Notes

Chapter Three   **Page 34**

"No Nation . . .": *New-York Weekly Journal*, November 19, 1733.

"A Monkey . . .": *New-York Weekly Journal*, December 10, 1733.

"A Large Spaneil . . .": *New-York Weekly Journal*, November 26, 1733.

"to provoke me . . .": letter from Cosby to Newcastle, December 17, 1733,
    Documents of New York, vol. 5, p. 974.

"I fear if . . .": *New-York Gazette*, January 28–February 4, 1733/34, found in Botein,
    Mr. Zenger's Malice.

"the Enjoyment of . . .": *New-York Weekly Journal*, April 1, 1734.

"'Tis not difficult . . .": *New-York Gazette*, April 8–15, 1734, found in Botein, *Mr. Zenger's Malice.*

"Some Men . . .": "The Charge of The Honourable James De Lancey, 15 January 1733,"
    Early American Imprints.

"was very generally disliked . . .": Colden, p. 321.

"infamous, agravated . . .": from the *New-York Gazette* as quoted in
    New-York Weekly Journal, April 1, 1734.

"the People of this Province . . .": *New-York Weekly Journal*, April 1, 1734.

"The Writers in that paper . . .": Colden, pp. 318–19.

Chapter Four   **Page 42**

"open and implacable . . .": letter from Cosby to Board of Trade, June 19, 1734,
    Documents of New York, vol. 6, p. 5.

"Tho' pettyfogging . . .": "Broadside: A Song made upon the foregoing occasion,"
    Early American Imprints.

"It is high time . . .": "The Charge of the Honourable James De Lancey, 15 October 1734,"
    Early American Imprints.

"view [New York's] Fortifications . . .": *New-York Weekly Journal*, December 17, 1733.

"since an Assembly . . .": quoted in *A Brief Narrative*, editor Finkelman, p. 84.

"It is ordered . . .": same as above, p. 88.

Chapter Five   **Page 50**

"excessive bail . . .": quoted in *A Brief Narrative*, editor Katz, p. 49.

"I [am] not worth forty . . .": same as above, p. 49.

"*To all my Subscribers* . . .": *New-York Weekly Journal*, November 25, 1734.

"Alterations were purposely . . .": *New-York Weekly Journal*, December 23, 1734.

"Matters of great . . .": *New-York Weekly Journal*, November 25, 1734.

Notes

Chapter Six   **Page 56**

"Publishing, Uttering . . .": Warrant for Bradford's arrest as quoted in Thomas, p. 344.

"false, malicious . . .": quoted in *A Brief Narrative*, editor Finkelman, p. 105.

"THE PEOPLE of this City . . .": *New-York Weekly Journal*, January 28, 1733/34.

"Consider the consequences . . .": quoted in *A Brief Narrative*, editor Katz, p. 52.

"*You have brought it* . . .": same as above, p. 53.

"With every Rain . . .": Peeck and Zenger, May 1, 1735.

Chapter Seven   **Page 64**

All trial quotations from *A Brief Narrative*, editor Katz.

"He had art, eloquence . . .": Smith, pp. 19–20.

"Defendant Zenger has pleaded . . .": p. 58.

"I'll save Mr. Attorney . . .": p. 62.

"Well Mr. Attorney . . .": p. 62.

"I think the jury . . .": p. 62.

"Not so . . .": p. 62.

"What is good . . .": pp. 67–68.

"We are ready . . .": p. 74.

"are notoriously known . . .": p. 75.

"No, Mr. Hamilton . . .": p. 78.

"If you should be of the opinion . . .": p. 96.

"The question before the Court . . .": p. 99.

"exposing and opposing . . .": p. 99.

"Not Guilty . . .": p. 101.

"scarcely one person . . .": Colden, p. 339.

"his Learned and generous . . .": quoted in *A Brief Narrative*, editor Finkelman, p. 166.

Chapter Eight   **Page 76**

"and ended . . .": Smith, p. 21.

"very good Friends . . .Paper War.": *New-York Gazette*, March 28, 1736, quoted in Botein,
    Mr. Zenger's Malice, p. 11.

"The trial of . . .": quoted in Rutherfurd, p. 131.

"THE FREEDOM OF SPEECH . . .": *Pennsylvania Gazette*, November 10 to 17, 1737, quoted in
    A Brief Narrative, editor Katz, p. 181.

Bibliography

Historical Documents

Alexander. James. *A Brief Narrative of the Case and Tryal of John Peter Zenger.* Edited with an introduction by Paul Finkelman. Union, NJ: The Lawbook Exchange, Ltd., 2000.

————. *A Brief Narrative of the Case and Trial of John Peter Zenger.* 2nd ed. Edited with an introduction by Stanley Nider Katz. Cambridge, MA: Belknap Press of Harvard University Press, 1972.

Botein, Stephen, ed. *'Mr. Zenger's Malice and Falshood,' Six Issues of the New-York Weekly Journal, 1733–34.* Includes excerpts from the *New-York Gazette.* Worcester, MA: American Antiquarian Society, 1985.

Boyd, Julian P., ed. *The Papers of Thomas Jefferson.* Vol. 11. Princeton, NJ: Princeton University Press, 1955.

Colden, Cadwallader. *History of William Cosby's Administration as Governor of the Province of New York and of Lieutenant-Governor George Clarke's Administration through 1737.* Cadwallader Colden Papers. Vol. IX. New York: The Collections of the New-York Historical Society, 1937.

Early American Imprints, Series I: Evans, 1639–1800. Readex Digital Collections, American Antiquarian Society and NewsBank, Inc., 2002.

O'Callaghan, E. B., ed. *Documents Relative to the Colonial History of the State of New-York.* Vols. 5 and 6. Albany, NY: Weed, Parsons, 1855.

Peeck, John, and John Peter Zenger. "Petition to City Council." City Council, 1647–1977. New York City Department of Records, Municipal Archives. http://www.nyc.gov/html/records/html/collections/collections_citycouncil.shtml.

Sheridan, Eugene R., ed. *The Papers of Lewis Morris.* Vol. II: 1731–1737. Newark: New Jersey Historical Society, 1993.

Whitehead, William A., ed. *Documents Relating to the Colonial History of the State of New Jersey.* Archives of the State of New Jersey, First Series. Vol. V. Newark, NJ: Daily Advertiser Printing House, 1882.

Zenger, John Peter, pub. *The New-York Weekly Journal,* 5 November 1733 through 18 March 1751.

Bibliography

Other References

Bailyn, Bernard. *The Ideological Origins of the American Revolution*. Cambridge, MA: Belknap Press of Harvard University Press, 1967.

———. *The Origins of American Politics*. New York: Alfred A. Knopf, 1968.

Bailyn, Bernard, and John B. Hench, eds. *The Press and the American Revolution*. Worcester, MA: American Antiquarian Society, 1980.

Bancroft, George. *History of the United States*. Vol. 2. New York: D. Appleton, 1883.

Bonomi, Patricia U. *A Factious People: Politics and Society in Colonial New York*. New York: Columbia University Press, 1971.

Botein, Stephen. *Early American Law and Society*. New York: Alfred A. Knopf, 1983.

Brown, James Wright. "Life & Times of John Peter Zenger." *Editors & Publishers*, 14, 21, and 28 March 1953 and 4, 11, and 18 April 1953.

Buranelli, Vincent. "The Myth of Anna Zenger." *William and Mary Quarterly*, April 1956, 157–168.

———, ed. *The Trial of Peter Zenger*. New York: New York University Press, 1957.

Burns, James MacGregor. *The Vineyard of Liberty*. New York: Alfred A. Knopf, 1982.

Copeland, David A. *Colonial American Newspapers: Character and Content*. Newark: University of Delaware Press, 1997.

Covert, Cathy. "Passion Is Ye Prevailing Motive: The Feud Behind the Zenger Case." *Journalism Quarterly*, Spring 1973, 3–10.

Drake, Francis S. *Dictionary of American Biography*. Boston: James R. Osgood, 1872.

Ferris, Robert G., ed. *The Presidents* (part of National Survey of Historic Sites and Buildings. Vol. 20). Washington, DC: U.S. Department of Interior, National Park Service, 1977.

Finkelman, Paul. "Politics, the Press, and the Law: The Trial of John Peter Zenger." In *American Political Trials*, edited by Michal R. Belknap, 25–44. Westport, CT: Greenwood Press, 1994.

Fleming, Thomas J. "A scandalous, malicious and seditious libel." *American Heritage* 19, no. 1 (December 1967): 22–27, 100–106.

Goebel, Julius, Jr., and T. Raymond Naughton. *Law Enforcement in Colonial New York, 1664–1776*. Montclair, NJ: Patterson Smith, 1970.

Harlan, Robert D. *The Colonial Printer*. UCLA: William Andrews Clark Memorial Library, 1978.

Hildeburn, Charles R. *Sketches of Printers and Printing in Colonial New York*. New York: Dodd, Mead, 1895.

Bibliography

Hoffer, Peter Charles. *Law and People in Colonial America*. Baltimore: Johns Hopkins University Press, 1992.

"John Peter Zenger: Truth Is a Defense." The Bill of Rights Institute, 2004. www.billofrightsinstitute.org.

Kammen, Michael. *Colonial New York: A History*. New York: Charles Scribner's Sons, 1975.

Katz, Stanley. *Newcastle's New York*. Cambridge, MA: Belknap Press of Harvard University Press, 1968.

Kemmerer, Donald L. *Path to Freedom: The Struggle for Self-Government in Colonial New Jersey*. Princeton, NJ: Princeton University Press, 1940.

Konkle, Burton Alva. *The Life of Andrew Hamilton*. Freeport, NY: Books for Libraries Press, 1972.

Labaree, Leonard Woods. *Royal Government in America*. New York: Frederick Ungar Publishing, 1958.

Lee, James Melvin. *History of American Journalism*. Garden City, NY: Garden City Publishing, 1923.

Levy, Leonard W. *Freedom of the Press from Zenger to Jefferson*. Indianapolis: Bobbs-Merrill, 1966.

Linder, Douglas. "The Trial of John Peter Zenger." *Jurist*, August 2001. jurist.law.pitt.edu/trials20.htm.

MacCracken, Henry Noble. *Prologue to Independence: The Trials of James Alexander, American, 1715–1756*. New York: James H. Heineman, 1964.

Marrin, Richard B. *A Glance Back in Time: Life in Colonial New Jersey (1704–1770) as depicted in News Accounts of the Day*. Bowie, MD: Heritage Books, 1994.

McConville, Bruce. *These Daring Disturbers of the Public Peace*. Ithaca, NY: Cornell University Press, 1999.

McCusker, John J. *How Much Is That in Real Money?* 2nd ed. Worcester, MA: American Antiquarian Society, 2001.

McKerns, Joseph P., ed. *Biographical Dictionary of American Journalism*. New York: Greenwood Press, 1989.

McMurtrie, Douglas C. *A History of Printing in the United States*. Vol. II. New York: Burt Franklin, 1969.

Moglen, Eben. "Considering Zenger: Partisan Politics and the Legal Profession in Provincial New York." Columbia Law School, 1998. Emoglen.law.columbia.edu/publications/zenger.html.

Morris, Richard Brandon. *Fair Trial*. New York: Harper and Row, 1967.

Bibliography

Oliver, The Honorable L. Stauffer. "The Origin of Pennsylvania's Present Day Courts in Early Colonial Times." Address given October 7, 1939. *Society of Colonial Wars in the Commonwealth of Pennsylvania*. Vol. 5, No. 3, 1939.

Oswald, John Clyde. *Printing in the Americas*. New York: Gregg Publishing, 1937.

Pasley, Jeffrey L. *The Tyranny of Printers*. Charlottesville: University of Virginia Press, 2001.

Phelps, Robert H., and E. Douglas Hamilton. *Libel*. New York: Macmillan, 1966.

Price, Warren C. "Reflections on the Trial of John Peter Zenger." *Journalism Quarterly* 32 (1955): 161–168.

Putnam, William Lowell. *John Peter Zenger and the Fundamental Freedom*. Jefferson, NC: McFarland, 1997.

Rutherfurd, Livingston, ed. *John Peter Zenger: His Press, His Trial, and a Bibliography of Zenger Imprints*. Gloucester, MA: Peter Smith, 1963.

Schlesinger, Arthur M. *Prelude to Independence: The Newspaper War on Britain, 1764–1776*. New York: Alfred A. Knopf, 1958.

Sheridan, Eugene R. *Lewis Morris, 1671–1746*. Syracuse, NY: Syracuse University Press, 1981.

Silver, Rollo G. *The American Printer, 1787–1825*. Charlottesville: The University Press of Virginia, 1967.

Singleton, Esther. *Social New York Under the Georges, 1714–1776*. New York: D. Appleton, 1902.

Smith, William, Jr. *The History of the Province of New-York*. Vols. 1 and 2. Edited by Michael Kammen. Cambridge, MA: Belknap Press of Harvard University Press, 1972.

Steers, B. MacDonald. *The Counsellors, Courts and Crimes of Colonial New York*. New York: Exposition Press, 1968.

Thomas, Isaiah. *The History of Printing in America*. Barre, MA: Imprint Society, 1970. Originally published 1810.

Todd, Charles Burr. *The Story of the City of New York*. New York: G. P. Putnam's Sons, 1902.

University of British Columbia, Sauder School of Business. Pacific Exchange Rate Service. http://Fx.sauder.ubc.ca.

Valentine, David T. *History of the City of New York*. New York: G. P. Putnam, 1853.

Williamson, Samuel H., ed. "How Much Is That?" Economic History.net. http://eh.net/hmit.

Wroth, Lawrence C. *The Colonial Printer*. Portland, ME: Southworth-Anthoensen Press, 1938.

Index

(Page numbers in *italics* refer to illustrations.)

Index

Index

Picture Credits

Dover Publications, Inc.: 56.

Copyright © 2005 **Alden Ford**: 70 (bottom), 78 (top right and bottom), 80 (bottom).

Library of Congress, Prints and Photographs Division, LC-USZ62-19360: 14; Library of Congress, Prints and Photographs Division, LC-USZ62-64702: 18 (top); Library of Congress, Prints and Photographs Division, Detroit Publishing Company Collection, LC-USZ62-48913: 32; Library of Congress, Prints and Photographs Division, LC-USZ62-38488: 40 (top left); Library of Congress, Prints and Photographs Division, LC-USZ62-120704: 46 (top); Library of Congress, Prints and Photographs Division, LC-USZ62-70245: 66; Library of Congress, Prints and Photographs Division, LC-USZ62-2566: 70 (top); Library of Congress, Prints and Photographs Division, LC-USZC2-6374: 72; Library of Congress, Prints and Photographs Division, LC-USA7-34630: 84 (top); Library of Congress, Prints and Photographs Division, LC-USZ62-63958: 84 (bottom).

Courtesy of **Morristown & Morris Township Library**: 28 (top).

Courtesy of **National Archives and Records Administration (NARA)**: 82.

Rare Books Division, **The New York Public Library**, Astor, Lenox and Tilden Foundations: 10; Print Collection, Miriam and Ira D. Wallach Division of Art, Prints and Photographs, The New York Public Library, Astor, Lenox and Tilden Foundations: 18 (bottom); Emmet Collection, Miriam and Ira D. Wallach Division of Art, Prints and Photographs, The New York Public Library, Astor, Lenox and Tilden Foundations: 20, 50, 78 (top left); I. N. Phelps Stokes Collection, Miriam and Ira D. Wallach Division of Art, Prints and Photographs, The New York Public Library, Astor, Lenox and Tilden Foundations: 30 (bottom); Picture Collection, The Branch Libraries, The New York Public Library, Astor, Lenox and Tilden Foundations: 36 (top), 42.

North Wind Picture Archives: 16, 48 (bottom), 68.

Courtesy **NYC Municipal Archives**: 62.

Reproduced with permission from **Readex, a division of NewsBank, Inc., and the American Antiquarian Society**: 6, 8, 12, 22, 24, 26, 28 (bottom), 30 (top), 36 (bottom left and right), 38, 40 (top right and bottom), 44 (both), 46 (bottom), 48 (top), 52, 54 (both), 58, 60, 64, 74, 76, 80 (top and middle).